Dear Aunt

May you have a healthy,
sweet, inspiring new year
filled with nachas and good
news.

It is wonderful to see you.

love,
Miriam

"**Tzvi Jacobs has the rare gift of writing with both heart and mind.** The finely crafted stories in *From the Heavens to the Heart* are gems of wisdom based on ordinary experience seen through the eyes of a man alert to the higher purpose of existence. Whether writing about Blanton, his anatomy class partner in Tennessee, or about Beryl, the little Hasidic boy run over by a taxi driver in New York, Jacobs has his eyes—and our attention—riveted on what is precious in the seemingly accidental unfolding of human events. He takes time to investigate carefully and record with insight actual happenings in which men, women and children reveal their Godly potential. To do this artfully and credibly at the end of the 20th century is no easy feat. Just as the author intended, the reader is left armed with a clearer vision for the revelations of truths yet to come. This is heartening in the deepest sense, without a trace of the maudlin. Simply delightful—and true."

Vera Schwarcz
Director/Chair, the Mansfield Freeman Center
for East Asian Studies, Wesleyan University
Author of *Bridge Across Broken Time:
Chinese and Jewish Cultural Memory*

from the Heavens to the Heart

true stories of extraordinary happenings
in the lives of ordinary people

by Tzvi Jacobs

From the Heavens to the Heart
True Stories of Extraordinary Happenings
in the Lives of Ordinary People
by Tzvi Jacobs

A pronunciation guide and illustrated glossary of Jewish terms
can be found at the back of the book

Request for information or additional books should be addressed to:
Tzvi Jacobs, 104 Sussex Avenue, Morristown, NJ 07960

ISBN: 0-9669610-0-5

Printed in Canada

Publisher's Cataloging-in-Publication
(Provided by Quality Books, Inc.)

Jacobs, Tzvi.
    From the heavens to the heart: true stories of
extraordinary happenings in the lives of
ordinary people / by Tzvi Jacobs. -- 1st ed.
    p. cm.
    LCCN: 99-70816
    ISBN: 0-9669610-0-5

    1. Jewish way of life--Anecdotes. 2. Jews--
Return to Orthodox Judaism--Anecdotes.
3. Habad--Anecdotes.   I. Title.

BM723.J33 2000   296.7'2
                           QBI99-1254

Book design and typesetting by
Yael Resnick, Superscript Communications, Morristown, New Jersey
Cover design by Nicholas Iannacone; artwork by Tim Jacobus
Graphic support by Triart Graphics, Cedar Knolls, New Jersey
Printed by LetroMac Design & Printing, Inc. Montreal, Canada
(Photo credits appear on page 207)

By the Grace of God
Yud Shvat 5760
January 17, 2000

Dear Reader,

From the heavens to the heart can be an infinite distance. Yet, we all strive to bridge that gap.

Back in 1969, I began my personal search for truth and meaning. Rather than trying to explain to you what I experienced and found, I will share with you the following true stories.

Because most of the stories center around Jewish characters and scenes (which I have been told appeal to everyone regardless of religious background or personal beliefs), I have added a pronunciation guide and an illustrated glossary to explain all of the Jewish terms.

Please read on and enjoy.

Shalom–Peace,

Tzvi Jacobs

TO MY FATHER

Yitzchak ben Aryeh Leib, of blessed memory,
known as Isaac Jacobs,
whose soul was called back to its Maker
on the 5th of Adar 5759 (February 21, 1999).
Thank you for your enthusiastic, unending support
and promoting of my stories.
I feel like you are still here,
encouraging me through the challenging times.

❧ Table of Contents ❧

∽ 1 ∾
Where the Moon Don't Shine

BACK IN 1974, during my college days at "Sewanee"— the University of the South in Sewanee, Tennessee—my buddies and I would occasionally escape the brightly lit library and sterile laboratories to head for the caves. Hidden within the untamed Cumberland Mountains were many primitive caves, conducive for clearing the mind of our rigorous studies.

On one such spelunking expedition, Blanton Miller, Mark Fockele and I jumped into Blanton's old, navy blue GM convertible and sped along the mountain roads to "moonshine country" in northern Alabama. After 30 minutes of driving, Blanton swung onto a blacktop and followed his handwritten map. The narrow road led to a gravel road, and that road led to a dirt road which led to an abandoned, overgrown firelane. We pushed the little car behind a bush, lest an enterprising local should spot the car and use the parts for a moonshine still.

We hiked up a deer path, took a right at the fork in the stream, and on the other side of a small hill, found the landmark: a huge boulder next to an equally large pit.

"This should be it," Blanton said, waving his map like a tattered flag.

"Where?" Mark and I asked at the same time.

"Between these rocks," mumbled Blanton, while deciphering his notes. "Dr. Caldwell said the entrance to the cave was on the eastern side of the boulder, at the base of a mound of smaller rocks." Dr. Hugh Caldwell might have been a professor of philosophy at Sewanee, but he certainly had explored more caves and ran more whitewater rapids than anyone we knew.

9

"I reckon it's down that hole," Blanton said, pointing to a two-foot wide space nestled between some rocks.

"Hey, guys, what are we waiting for!" Mark said, jumping to his feet. He pulled out of his canvas backpack three caving helmets and passed them around. Each of us locked a small carbide lantern onto the front "forehead" of his helmet. I watched Blanton as he carefully opened a nozzle at the base of his lantern's water chamber. Water from this upper chamber dripped into the lower chamber of volatile carbide granules. After a two-second delay, the water and carbide reacted and produced a gas, which hissed as it pushed its way through a nozzle in the middle of the lantern's reflector disk. A round, metal striker, like the kind on a cigarette lighter, was mounted next to the gas nozzle. Blanton flicked the striker and the gas ignited into a bright, pointy flame.

"Okay, let's go," Blanton said, as he strapped the helmet onto his head, pushing back his wavy red hair. He got onto his knees and slithered through the slit, disappearing into the darkness.

"Hey, guys, this looks like it," his voice rose from the abyss. Mark and I followed, crawling along some muddy ground. Immediately, we were in another world, another century. The Viet Nam War no longer existed, getting into a top law school vanished from Mark's consciousness, deciding about going to medical school from mine.

The hole expanded, wider and taller, and within a minute or two, we were able to walk upright on broken layers of rock. After 15 minutes or so of winding downwards, Blanton stopped.

"Wow! I'll be," he said, his Manchester, Tennessee, accent coming strong and clear. A huge room of icicle-shaped stalactites, hanging from the cavern's roof, opened before us.

Fearlessly, Blanton leapt to the rock below and let out a "whoopie" which echoed back to him.

"Careful, you dancing dryad," Mark said. Mark possessed a sophisticated vocabulary, sprinkled with terms from classical literature. After all, his father published the daily newspaper in Gainesville, Georgia.

Mark and I inched down the rocks and stood on the floor of the room. Following Mark's cue, I removed my helmet and increased the dripping of the water to make the flame bigger. I was awestruck at the intricate architecture of this cathedral-like room.

Swoosh. I jumped. A faint, yet distinct, sound had whirred past my head. "What's that?"

"A bat," Blanton yelled. "Look, there's more!"

Our eyes focused on the high ceiling. Four or five bats swooped around in the air, probably sizing up the intruders with their radar vision. It was a strange, spooky world, where "birds" were flying rodents.

"Hey, guys, I think I found a tunnel," Blanton called out from the other side of the cavernous room. Back on our bellies, we crawled deeper, down into the mountain. The tunnel got narrower, but there was still room to drag our bodies through. Who knows what one would find at the end of one of these tunnels? It certainly was not a place for the weak-hearted or claustrophobic. After about 15 minutes...

Sputter, sputter.

Mark stopped and listened. Again, he heard a sound coming from above: *Sputter, sputter, sput.*

"Oh, fiddlesticks!" Mark cursed. Mark never used actual curse words. His refined father instilled that wholesome trait into his son.

"Are you out of water?" Blanton called back.

Mark unbuckled his helmet, detached the carbide lantern, and shook it.

Swoosh.

"Darn it!" Mark continued. "It has water. It sounds like it's out of carbide."

"No wonder. Your lantern was boiling faster than a moonshine still," Blanton said, with a spontaneous laugh.

Mark's water chamber had been dripping mighty fast and rapidly depleted the carbide.

"Don't worry, two lanterns are plenty. Squeeze around Herb and you'll have my light in front of you and Herb's behind you."

We continued crawling, and the path got narrower.

Sputter, sputter, sputter.

The tunnel became dimmer and dimmer, and then suddenly, it was dark. For crying out loud!

"Wait up guys. I think my lantern's out," I called out.

"Herb, you too?" Mark said, as he craned his neck over his shoulder to verify that my flame was gone.

"Blanton, we better turn around," Mark said, his voice rising. Not waiting for an answer, Mark pressed himself against the wall to see if he could contort his body, but the hole we were crawling through was too narrow. It was not a good time or a good place to panic. Or to have an asthma attack. My chest already felt tight. I closed my eyes and told myself not to freak out. Relax, breathe slowly. The walls left scant inches on either side of us, and from the floor to the ceiling was only a foot and a half.

"There's no turning around now," Blanton said. "Let's go a bit further and see if this tunnel gets wider. Don't worry, I've got plenty of fuel. Besides, I packed a flashlight. Do you want me to get it out?"

"No, thanks," Mark and I cried in unison. Crawling with a flashlight in one hand was very awkward. We followed Blanton's darkened figure, hoping the tunnel would soon widen. This is crazy, the thought popped in my head. No it's not, I argued back. Life is an adventure, and the only power that can stop one from enjoying it is fear. And what's the power of fear? Nothing. Just a shadow of darkness. And darkness is nothing, too.

Sputter, sputter, sputter, sputter.

My heart pounded against the ribs of my chest. Dim images of the brown, rugged walls flashed on and off. Then darkness, only darkness. No, it was more than darkness: absolute blackness.

For a minute, the darkness absorbed all sound.

"Wow, this is awesome," Blanton's voice rolled through the blackness.

"Real cool," Mark said, sarcastically. "Blanton, have you seen enough darkness? I prefer to see a little light."

"Don't worry, we still have a flashlight," sang Blanton, while rocking back and forth, shimmying his pack off his back.

12

"Uh, oh," Blanton's muffled voice said. Then came the familiar sound of someone opening a flashlight and sliding batteries in and out. Mark and I waited in suspense.

"Anyone got matches?" Blanton finally asked.

"Nope," I answered. I checked my pockets just in case.

"Darn it!" Mark said. "I can't believe I didn't bring matches." A former Boy Scout, Mark hated being unprepared.

"Next time," Blanton said, with a single chuckle.

"What should we do now?" I asked. I was a city boy. When it came to the outdoors, Blanton served as my mentor.

Blanton unstrapped his helmet, and shook his lantern.

"Hmmm. There's plenty of carbide in my lantern," said Blanton. "Plenty of water, too."

Mark and I sat silently in the darknesss, trying not to think of the danger we were in.

"I hear the water dripping," Blanton continued, in a calm voice, as if he were working on an experiment in the chemistry lab. "But I don't feel any gas coming out."

Blanton never lost his cool. His father, "Red" Blanton, always told him, "Blanton, if you're ever in a situation that you don't know what to do, just stay calm." His father had plenty of practice: he fought in World War II in some very bloody battles.

In our junior year at Sewanee, Blanton and I became anatomy lab partners. For me, it was a somewhat unpleasant struggle finding and memorizing the dozens of muscles and their insertions and origins, and every organ in between. Blanton stayed constantly upbeat, amazed at the beautiful intricacies and unfathomable wisdom of our cat's cadaver. Somehow death did not scare him; perhaps because he considered it another part of life, the final cave to explore.

But not yet. This world had much more to offer. Blanton dreamed of visiting Russia and wanted to learn how to use the electron microscope.

Another long minute passed. Mark and I were silent, lost in our thoughts of doom. Then, I heard the unstrapping of a helmet and carbide rattling in a lantern.

"The gas valve must be clogged," Blanton said, sealing the verdict.

Thud! Someone kicked the ground with real anger.

"Shishkabob! I can't believe I didn't bring matches!" Mark was a perfectionist. Even at Sewanee, where bright students had to work hard for a "B," Mark had a 4.0—straight "A"s.

Blanton gave the orders. "Okay, crawl backwards, guys. We can get back to the big room without light."

Crawling backwards was not an easy feat. The tunnel curved and twisted, something I didn't notice so much when crawling forward in the light. Every once in a while, Mark's boot would bang into my fingers. I could not see my own hand, let alone his boots backing into me. "Sorry, Herb," he would say each time, with sincerity. Mark never forgot his manners.

We were in real trouble. We could make it to the big room, but the small opening for the tunnel which would lead us to the outside was somewhere on the other side of the room. To find it in utter darkness would be next to impossible. Most likely, we would end up getting more lost. Or hurt on the rocks. I was wondering what the papers would write about us.

Three promising students of the University of the South, disappeared on Saturday...

The ceiling finally got higher, the walls got wider. We made it to the large room, bathed in total darkness.

"Blanton?" I asked.

"Yup."

"Did you tell anyone where we were going?"

"Nope. Didn't know myself."

If we only had one match, we could light one of our shirts.

Swoosh, swoosh.

"I never envied a bat 'til now," Mark said, morosely.

This underground temple which we had discovered two hours earlier—with its massive stalactites hanging from the high ceiling, and the dozens of stalagmites rising from the floor, like lifeless figures shrouded in mud—had become our dungeon.

Mark didn't have to tell me he was frightened; I could hear it in his cracking voice. I was scared out of my wits, too. We needed to pray—but to whom? Mark had debunked religion a long time ago, believing there was no way to prove that a supreme being existed. Two or three days a year I attended services for the High Holidays, out of obligation, not out of faith. But in the scary darkness of that cave, I prayed… just in case Someone would hear.

Ping. A solitary drop of water fell on the rocky ground, somewhere across the sea of darkness.

Then came a closer sound—the sound of a plastic bag crinkling. Afterwards, I heard the faint sound of paper being torn.

"Blanton, is that you tearing something?" I asked.

"Yup, Herb. I'm stripping the paper off this twist tie. Anybody care for a peanut butter and jelly sandwich?"

"Let's wait. We might have to ration the sandwiches," I said, nervously.

A minute later we all heard a hissing sound. A shiver shook my spine. Snakes in the dark are especially scary. The hiss was interrupted by the familiar raspy sound of the metal lantern striker. *Rrrasp.*

Light! The striker emitted a spark and ignited the hissing gas. A tiny arrow of fire vibrated in the center of the lantern's reflector disk.

"Thank goodness!" Mark exclaimed.

"We better make a run for it," Blanton said, already climbing over the rocks. Moving faster than one should, we scurried across the room and found the tunnel that led us to the outside.

A smiling Blanton pushed back his wavy red hair and held up the thin wire in the sunlight which he had stripped from the twist tie. He had used this tiny wire to unclog the gas valve, just enough for the gas to seep through and give us a tiny flame.

Blanton leapt off the rock. "Thank God for this wire!" he shouted to the trees.

Source: Mrs. Harry G. Miller, mother of Blanton, may he rest in peace; Mark Fockele, Esq.; Tzvi (Herb) Jacobs.

~2~
Flipping Over

O N A SUNNY AFTERNOON IN JUNE 1981, 25-year-old Allan Goldstein hopped onto his motorcycle and whizzed along the hilly suburban streets of Columbia, South Carolina. Rain had drenched the city earlier that morning, but the hot Carolina sun had come out and quickly dried the streets.

Riding was fun. Allan had bought the motorcycle only a month earlier, yet he rode it like a pro, whipping in and out of traffic. To keep bugs from flying in his eyes, the perfect-sighted Allan had put on eyeglasses. But a helmet, no way! He was too macho for that.

Allan swung onto Forrest Drive and raced downhill, zooming in behind a big truck. A large, leafy branch stretched over the street. The high roof of the truck swatted the wet branch and a hoard of water droplets were flung through the air. While the droplets were still in flight, the traffic light at the bottom of the hill turned red and the truck driver hit the brakes. A spray of water pelted Allan's eye glasses, and fogged his vision. Everything stopped except the blinded Allan, who was speeding downhill straight for the truck's shiny rear.

Losing his balance, Allan and his motorcycle spilled onto the road and skidded forward. His handsome face had just missed meeting the truck's rear fender. The truck driver heard the sound of metal scraping and crunching under his truck. He jumped out of the cabin and looked underneath the truck bed. A mangled motorcycle was wedged against the rear axle. He walked to the back of the truck, expecting the worst.

A guy crawled out, his windbreaker in shreds. He touched his head, chest and arms. "Sonny, are you okay?" the trucker asked, his eyes bulging.

"I think so, I feel okay," Allan said. "Yes, thank God, I'm fine." He suffered no injuries, not even a scratch. The motorcycle, of course, was totaled.

No more motorcycles for Allan. Instead, he used the insurance money and bought a motorboat. Falling on water seemed much safer. One beautiful day in July, Allan took a couple of friends out on Lake Murray, one of the largest lakes in South Carolina. His friend Herb "dropped" a ski in the water while attempting to slalom. After Herb climbed back into the boat, Allan spotted the missing ski and dived into the lake. Unencumbered by a life jacket, he effortlessly swam the 100 yards to the ski.

Reaching the ski, Allan lifted it up like a trophy. Then, "Owww!" he screamed. It sounded like a shark had bit him. But Herb and Rachel knew better—Lake Murray was 100 miles from the ocean. Allan was always joking around.

"Just a charley horse," Allan shouted after a long pause. "It's nothing, just need to rest a minute." He wrapped his left arm around the ski and massaged his shin with his right hand.

"Owww!" he screamed again. Allan grabbed his cramping shin with both hands, letting go of the half-submerged ski. The released ski sprung into the air and whacked the back of his head on the nape of the neck. Just like in the cartoons, Allan's right hand shot up, pointing to the sky, and followed him as he sunk straight down.

Rachel and Herb looked at each other in shock. She dived into the lake and swam towards the spot where Allan had sunk. Herb hadn't driven a boat for more than ten years. He turned the ignition key and pushed the gear handle. The boat jerked forward. At full speed, Herb raced to the area where Allan had gone under. It was the middle of the lake, and the water was choppy and deep. Time was ticking away and Allan was still nowhere in sight.

Breathing hard, Rachel reached the area and plunged frantically below the surface. Herb circled the boat around the area. Once, twice, three times.

"Whoaa!" a voice gasped from the waters behind the boat. It was Allan!

Herb stopped the boat and pulled in Allan's limp body. For literally five minutes the three of them could not speak.

"I saw the Angel of Death," panted Allan. "Herb, you were dragging me behind the boat."

"Dragging you?" Herb asked.

"I don't know how it happened, but the ski rope got wrapped around my ankle. It jolted me back to consciousness, but then you kept dragging me under the water."

"But I was circling the area looking for you," said Herb.

"Well, I was drowning all over again," Allan said. "I used every bit of strength that I had to reach up and grab the rope—it was wound tightly around this ankle." Allan's ankle was still red. "I don't know how I did it, but I pulled on that rope with all my might, just enough to slip my foot through."

Herb pulled in the ski rope. The outer threads of the section of rope which had been wound around Allan's ankle were split like frizzy hair.

Two weeks later Allan sold his boat. "It's just a toy," he said. Besides he could use the money to make payments on his new Toyota Cressida, which he had bought at the beginning of the summer.

Life was quiet... for a month. Then, on a clear, quiet Sunday night in August, a truck driver was cruising an 18-wheeler along State Highway 321 towards Columbia. As he crossed over Interstate-26, he glanced a bit ahead at a car veering off the interstate onto the Cayce-Columbia exit ramp. "That's a right tight curve," the trucker said to himself. "He better slow dowww..."

SCREEEECH!!! KABOOOM!

"Oh, my God," the trucker gasped.

A small car flipped and rolled—one, two, three times—on the concrete exit ramp. The silver car landed upside down on the edge of the ramp. The truck driver grabbed his CB, pulled over, and radioed the highway patrol. "Car flipped over on Cayce exit, I-26 West. Saw driver and one passenger."

"Yup," the trucker answered. "Looks like they touched ground for the last time."

The highway patrol immediately dispatched two ambulances. The trucker stared through the window, feeling too sick to move. The squashed car looked like a crumpled pie tin with wheels on top, still spinning, stirring the thick, hot August air. One of the front wheels was out of sync, its tire having been blown wide open.

A minute later, a flashing, screaming patrol car arrived at the scene. The patrol officer ran to the car and shined his flashlight through the narrow, jagged opening where the driver's window had been. A young man was already at the scene signaling traffic, waving a flashlight around the crushed car.

"Where are the bodies? Where's the driver?" the officer shouted to the citizen directing traffic.

"Bodies? Here," said the smiling young man, pointing to himself, "I'm the driver."

"Are you okay?" the officer asked.

"Thank God. Yes, thank God! See?" Allan said, as he turned around, lifting his arms up and down. "Not a scratch."

"How about the passenger?" the officer asked. "We were told there was a passenger."

"She's over there on the grass. Just a bump on the head," Allan said. "The automatic seat belts tightened on impact, and held us in our seats."

"Boy, you're a mighty lucky fellow," said the officer, shaking his head in disbelief.

While waiting for the tow truck, Allan used the pay phone at the gas station next to the exit ramp. "Herb, are you sitting down?"

"Yeh, I'm sitting at the computer working on my thesis," Herb said. Herb was studying towards a master's degree in public health epidemiology at the University of South Carolina.

Allan told Herb about his car flipping over. "And both of you are okay?!" Herb said. "I don't know what the probability is of three near fatal accidents happening in three months to one person, but it sounds way beyond random chance. I don't know, maybe you better write that Rebbe of yours."

Flipping Over

When Allan got home, he wrote a letter to the Lubavitcher Rebbe. Allan was not a bearded, black-hatted chassid, but he had visited the Rebbe many times and knew enough about him to know that the Rebbe possessed a special vision to see beyond the physical limits of this world.

The following morning, Allan was about to walk out of his apartment to mail the letter to the Rebbe... The phone rang. "Allan, my father has been trying to reach you," said Rabbi Yossi Groner, the Lubavitch emissary in Charlotte, North Carolina. Rabbi Groner's father served as a secretary to the Rebbe. "The Rebbe said you should check your *tefillin* [prayer boxes]."

Allan stared at his hand—the unmailed letter to the Rebbe was still in it. Taking heed of the Rebbe's advice, that afternoon Allan mailed his tefillin to a *sofer* [scribe] in Brooklyn. The scribe snipped the threads that had sealed the leather tefillin boxes shut, lifted out the parchments that were rolled and folded inside each of the two boxes, and carefully examined each letter written on the parchments.

Allan's tefillin were visibly new. His father had bought them in Israel in the spring, and Allan set aside his old pair of tefillin, which he had worn daily since his *bar mitzvah*, and started wearing the new ones at the beginning of the summer. Afterwards commenced his "transportation problems."

A week later Allan got a call from the scribe. He told Allan the tefillin were *posul* [invalid]. Entire words were missing from the parchments and he would have to get new parchments.

Thanks to the Rebbe's "insight," by the end of the summer Allan was praying with *kosher* tefillin and life became much safer.

Today, eighteen years later, Allan and Rachel are happily married with six beautiful children. Allan now drives a minivan, sports a beard and a *yarmulke*, and has a scribe check his tefillin every summer.

Sources: Tzvi (Herb) Jacobs; Jimmy Campbell, South Carolina Department of Transportation, Engineering Division; "Allan" and "Rachel" are fictitious names.

৵3৵
Waking Up

BACK IN THE SUMMER OF 1982, when black strands stilldominated his long, untrimmed beard, Rabbi Avrohom Lipskier would sit down every Thursday night with the students in his yeshiva. It was a time for sharing *Torah* thoughts, searching one's soul, and lively singing.

Ultimately, it was a time for nourishing and reviving our hidden Godly souls. Most of us *Baalei Teshuvah* had been far from the path of Torah and *mitzvahs* and had only recently begun to discover that we even had a soul, let alone a Godly soul. We'd make some *l'chaim*s to open our hearts and convince our coarse "animal" souls to lie down and let our Godly souls emerge. Such a process could not be rushed or forced by the hands of a clock. Sometimes nothing would seem like it was getting through our "grub" souls. But if one stayed up late enough and drank enough *Chassidic* teachings...

"There was once a Jew," said Rabbi Lipskier, with a raspy voice and a mischievous smile, "who thought he was so holy because he learned Torah all day. Not only did he learn Torah all day, but for 40 days he did not speak any *devarim betailim*—idle talk. He read that if a person doesn't speak idle talk for 40 days, he will merit to see Eliyahu Hanavi, you know, Elijah the Prophet. Well, he didn't see nuthin', so he travelled to the *Baal Shem Tov* to find out what happened. Before he could ask his question, the Baal Shem Tov said to a horse, within earshot of this 'holy' Jew: "My, you're such a holy horse. You haven't spoken any idle talk for 40 days."

I always thought of myself as refined and educated. After all, I had graduated from the University of the South, "Sewanee," one of the best liberal arts colleges in the country. On top of that, I had recently earned a master's degree in Public Health. I resisted

23

the implied slight to my character and intelligence. Throughout the night, I listened with an "open mind" to Rabbi Lipskier's words, but inside I was kicking and stamping and saying "neigh" to his words.

Then, a "miracle" happened. I realized I was a horse... a Carolina stallion, still doing everything, with a pile of hay in mind. It was a shocking revelation to me.

At the climax of the gathering, we sang and danced in a circle, Chassidic-style, and pranced our Rabbi home. The hidden sun cast its light onto the black sky and revealed a subdued blue above us. Dawn was quickly approaching. With inspired joy, I said the *Shema*—"Hear O Israel, the Lord is our God, the Lord is One." I felt very happy to be learning in Rabbi Lipskier's yeshiva.

As I "*plotzed*" onto my bed for a blissful sleep, the warm light of the Chassidic stories and teachings caressed my thoughts. A pleasant mixture of cake and vodka brought a smile to my stomach. With such a sweet brew, I knew I could sleep late.

Unlike every Sunday through Thursday, during which we had classes from 7:30 A.M. until 9:30 P.M., the focus on Fridays was outreach—to visit the sick or the elderly, or see our regular 'clientele' of Jewish business people, lawyers and others and share a word of Torah and promote the wearing of *tefillin* or the lighting of the Sabbath candles.

So, after that all-nighter, I went to sleep, planning to say the morning prayers late and go on my outreach route in the afternoon.

"*Boker tov* [good morning]! Everybody *up!!!* It's almost nine o'clock!" a student with the voice of a drill sergeant announced. Oh, no, it was Rafi.

"Come on, Yankel. It's almost time to say *Shema*," he said to the guy in the cot next to mine, while shaking his corpse-like body back and forth.

"Tzvi, wake up. It's time to say *Shema*," he boomed in my face.

My eyes would not open. "I already said *Shema*," I muttered. "I need sleep."

Waking Up

Yeshiva students at a farbrengen

Thank God, he left the room! I could hear his *bang, bang, bang* on each of the dozen dorm rooms that were up and down the hall, shouting, "Everyone up. It's time to say *Shema*. Get up. It's *mivtzoyim* [outreach] day."

I wanted to say, "If you were at the *farbrengen*..." and then I remembered that he was also at the gathering with Rabbi Lipskier till the end.

Oh, no, he returned. "Nu, Shmuely, wake up," Rafi barked at the Argentinian student on the other side of my room.

Who does this fired-up Israeli think he is coming into our room and waking us up? Does he think we're in the army?!

My bed was next to an open window. A soft, summer breeze gently brushed across my face. It smelled of the fresh tree-covered foothills surrounding Morristown, New Jersey.

"I'm right, right?" I asked myself, as I began to fall back into deep sleep. Then, a thought caught me as I tottered on the brink of consciousness.

"I wonder what the Rebbe would say?" I said in my head.

Half a second passed. *BZZZZZZZZZZZZZ.* The sound of a bee entered from the direction of the open window.

My left eye lid lifted a crack. The bee headed across my bed, made a quick loop, and shot into the fleshy flesh between my thumb and index finger.

"OWWWWWWW!"

I jumped up, feet on the floor. I quickly splashed water onto my hands. The sting was already swelling and hurting. I ran to my narrow closet and grabbed the Arm & Hammer baking powder, which served as my toothpaste in those days. Quickly, I patted the powder onto my damp hand.

My sleepiness had vanished.

By the time I got to the *bais midrash* and wrapped the *tefillin* around my left hand, I noticed the swelling of the bee sting was totally down. The only trace was a tiny hole.

I laughed. I guess the Rebbe gave this horse an answer: "Wake up, *Yidele!*"

❧ 4 ❧
The Rebbe's Advice

*D*on't you know someone your sister can meet?"
It was September 1983 and I had five sisters, but I knew that Dad was talking about my older. Susan was living near my parents' home in Charleston, and had attended all of the Jewish singles gatherings in South Carolina.

"You must know somebody."

I dropped a folded shirt into the suitcase and sighed. "It's hard to find a single guy up North to travel to South Carolina to meet someone. And then when I tell them she has two children, they're even less interested. But, remember, I brought that guy down with me this past Passover."

"Why, he didn't even have a steady job. How's someone with a new sales job every six weeks supposed to support a wife and two children?"

"I guess not…"

Dad always worried too much about money, and I rebelled against it. I always made enough to get by. Savings accounts and financial planning were not in my vocabulary. Even though I was 29, I jumped straight from graduate school to yeshiva, where all the basic necessities—food, shelter, and donated clothing—came to us like *manna* from Heaven.

Dad, however, earned his degree in the College of Hard Knocks. In 11th grade, he contracted a severe mastoid infection in his left ear and was unable to return to high school. The year was 1933; the Depression Era had sunk in. Dad joined the CCC (the Civilian Conservation Corps) and built paths and bridges in state parks. He sent his money home to help his parents support his seven other siblings. No wonder Dad always quoted the saying "hard work never hurt anybody."

27

"That rabbi in Charlotte must know some single men," Dad said.

"Rabbi Groner said he'd keep his eyes open."

Last winter I had arranged for Susan to spend the weekend at the Chabad House of Rabbi and Yossi and Mariasha Groner in Charlotte, North Carolina. Susan went with her children and became close with the Groner's other sleepover guests, Miriam Schoenes and her husband Boruch. Susan was inspired by their return to traditional Judaism as well the experience of spending the entire Sabbath at the Chabad House. Well, she found some true peace that Sabbath, but no husband to share it with.

"Maybe you can write the Rebbe. I just heard a story about an older couple who asked the Rebbe for a blessing for their only daughter to find her *beshert* (intended match) and the Rebbe..."

"I pray to God! I don't pray to no rebbe!" Dad blurted out.

I jumped, startled like a scared deer, and saw my father's lips still trembling. My breath was caught on a snag in my throat and I stood frozen. Dad lifted his hand and was about to say something, but turned in silence and paced towards the couch.

During the past year, my first year in yeshiva, I had told him many stories about the Lubavitcher Rebbe, to which he always respectfully listened. I had no idea that he was bothered by these stories. Dad himself attended the Orthodox synagogue in Charleston, the one which his great-grandfather founded in 1854. However, the Chassidic tradition of a rebbe was foreign to him.

I zipped up my suitcase and glanced across at Dad, who was now seated on the couch, his face buried in a newspaper. Life was definitely tough for Dad—my oldest sister leaving a bad marriage and escaping with her two children, my brother suffering from frequent bouts of manic-depression, a daughter in college, and the youngest, who was only 14, attending a costly Jewish parochial school. Although Dad was 66, he couldn't afford to retire. I guess the thought of a 29-year-old son who attended an elite private college and who had almost finished graduate school but now was heading up North to seclude himself in some yeshiva—this must have also cast a shadow of darkness to his already darkened picture. As upset as he was, Dad was also exhausted. He slumped down into the couch, his chin resting on his chest, softly snoring. I slipped out of the living room and sat down in the kitchen.

Mom was cutting carrots on the chopping board, and slid them into a pot of boiling water with a chicken bobbing up and down. She had evidently heard my exchange with Dad, because she then filled me in. "Last year, a rabbi from New York gave a lecture at the Jewish Community Center. After the lecture, Dad approached him and told him that you had recently dropped out of graduate school and escaped into a 'Loobavitch' yeshiva. Your Dad asked him, 'What is this Loobavitch group? I've never heard of it.' "

"So what did the rabbi answer?"

"He said that he wouldn't call it a cult, but they do have this charismatic rabbi, whom they call the Rebbe, who is an intermediary between his followers and God, like the Pope.

"The rabbi then said, 'Praying to an intermediary, you probably know, is not a Jewish concept.' "

"What! That's what that rabbi said?" I jumped. I felt my face flush and turn warm. "Throughout Jewish history, whenever someone's prayers weren't answered, they would always turn to a *tzaddik*, a holy person, and ask for a blessing. Why, people even come up to me, seeing me in a black hat and beard, and say, 'Rabbi, please pray for my son,' or 'Please bless my lottery ticket.' But I don't think anyone would ever say that they're praying to me!"

I was livid. And I knew I shouldn't be. I must have been uncomfortable with the idea myself of the chassidim's adoration of the Rebbe. When I first came to Crown Heights a year and a half earlier, I was uncomfortable with seeing pictures of the Rebbe everywhere. And it seemed as if everybody wrote the Rebbe asking for his blessing before they did or bought anything. But during that year in yeshiva, I saw how he Rebbe was like a Moses in our generation, how he was bringing Heaven down to earth, and connecting earthlings to Heaven, to a deep and true belief in God.

For a long time, I sat silently in my mother's kitchen, my thoughts boiling faster than the chicken soup.

Mom finally broke the silence. "Well, I hope your Rebbe is praying that they accept your thesis," she said with a nervous laugh.

"I'm sure he is, because he knows I need to return to yeshiva. Don't worry. My professors seemed pleased with it when I defended it last week. Besides, they want to see me graduate already."

The following morning I drove back to Morristown, New Jersey, to learn for maybe another year in yeshiva. During that two-day drive, I had no tape player and plenty of time to think. Every generation has a Moses-like leader, at least that's what the Chabad-Lubavitch rebbes teach. For sure, having a Moses-figure was a Jewish concept. There was Abraham, then Isaac, followed by Jacob, and Joseph in Egypt. After Moses, Joshua led the people. And then the kings. Even more recently, there were leaders like Rashi and Maimonides who stood out in their respective generations.

When I arrived at yeshiva, I had a letter waiting for me. Three sheets, back and front, in Dad's unmistakable script. Dad wanted to know when I was going to use my degree. "You don't want to be a traveling salesman like me." For the past 45 years and still spinning, Dad pushed the pedal of his station wagon, five days a week, lugging his sample cases of hosiery, underwear, and other "dry goods" to merchants throughout the small towns of South Carolina. It was tough job, and now he wrote as if it were all for naught. Dad sounded really down, like he had been a failure. Dad ended the letter: "Please find a nice Jewish man for Susan. Love, Dad."

There were some new guys in yeshiva. Since this yeshiva was for Jewish men who had little or no background in Jewish learning and observance, there were always new faces—kids who came before going to college, others during and after college, and some older in the midst of some transition or revelation or crisis. However, at that time, except for two men who were probably in their 50s, all of the other guys in yeshiva were between 17 and 25, with the exception of me and Shmuel, who was close to 30.

He seemed too observant for Susan, but still I asked him. "I'm not looking," he said, without even taking his eyes off the page of the Talmud.

I was inspired by what I was learning in yeshiva, especially the Chassidic teachings and, of course, the "Rebbe stories,"so I continued to write Dad weekly letters, as if nothing was ever said.

One of my teachers in yeshiva was Rabbi Yeheskel Lebovic, who with his wife served also as a *shadchan*, or matchmaker. I told him about Susan. "Ask her to come to New York and we'll introduce her to someone."

Susan had a vacation during the last week of December. (She had worked herself up from secretary level to being a nuclear submarine technician at the Charleston Naval Shipyard.) She followed Rabbi Lebovic's advice and made reservations to fly to New York.

One day when I called home, I was shocked when my father read me the opening paragraph of a letter: "Dear Rebbe, My son Tzvi said I should write you and ask you to pray that my eldest daughter Raizel Shoshana bas Rivkah marry a nice Jewish man..." Dad said he was enclosing a donation of $18.

About a month later, Dad was suffering from heartburn. He took some antacid, but the pains in his chest intensified. Mom drove Dad to the emergency room. He had had a heart attack, but thank God, he received treatment in time. While in the hospital that week, Dad received a letter from the Rebbe, dated the 3rd of Teves, 5744 (December 9, 1983):

Greeting and Blessing:
I received your letter of Nov. 9th with some delay. As requested, I will remember you in prayer for the fulfillment of your heart's desires for good in regard to yourself and the other members of your family.
There is surely no need to explain to you at length that all blessings come from God, and the channel to receive them is through the everyday

life and conduct in accordance with His Will. Therefore, every additional effort in matters of Torah and Mitzvoth, though a must for their own sake, widens these channels.

It is also well to bear in mind that all members of a Jewish family constitute one entity, one body, where a benefit to one part is a benefit to all. Hence, an extra effort in Yiddishkeit on the part of one member of the family, especially parents, benefits each and all members of the family.

Receipt is enclosed for your Tzedoko, and may it bring you and yours additional Divine blessings.

With blessing, [signed] M. Schneerson

Mom mailed me a copy of the Rebbe's letter and I studied it. Dad had not asked the Rebbe that bothersome question of "Is the Rebbe an intermediary?"—and yet the Rebbe had answered the question in his letter. He reassured Dad, who knew with an enviable simple faith, that "all blessings come from God." Now, God, who desires to shower his creatures with goodness and kindness, gives generous blessings … but they are not always received. The Rebbe then explained how blessings are received from God. Blessings come through "channels." These channels are created by living our daily life in "in accordance with His Will" and "Every additional effort in matters of Torah and Mitzvoth, though a must for their own sake, widens these channels."

"An extra effort in Yiddishkeit on the part of one member of the family, especially parents, benefits each and all members of the family." In this sense, everyone is an "intermediary," a channel to direct blessings from God to others to whom one is close. Is the Rebbe simply serving as a spiritual father, connecting his children to God?

On December 22, Susan flew to New York. I arranged for her to spend *Shabbos* with some friends in Crown Heights, Rabbi Shmuel and Sterna Spritzer.

"I got a blessing from the Rebbe to meet my husband-to-be."

The Spritzers smiled. They didn't have the heart to tell her that they knew many young women who had received blessings from the Rebbe to meet their intended. Not just one blessing but many, and they had been looking for years. They live in New York City—they're not just visiting for a week—and are fully observant, have never been married, and don't have any children. But Susan had pure trust in the Rebbe's blessing.

Three matchmakers had been contacted, and each lined up a date for her for the coming week. Susan didn't like the first two dates she met, but things clicked with the third one. The chemistry was good. In fact, Avi was finishing a master's degree in chemistry at Johns Hopkins University in Baltimore. The two kept in touch with each other and with their matchmakers, Rabbi Yeheskel and Pearl Lebovic.

In the spring of 1984, Susan and Avi became engaged and were married in the summer.

My father followed the Rebbe's advice and increased in his observance of Torah and *mitzvos,* and blessings began to flow. Dad's spirits had picked up, his health improved, and the year after Susan married, three more of his children married during the following three years. Channels of blessings were now growing wider and wider, flowing sweeter and sweeter. Even I became more or less a *mensch* and accepted a real job in the pharmaceutical industry. "Keep writing your stories, Tzvi. Just don't quit your day job."

It became obvious to many that Dad had received a special blessing, and God was shining a warm, loving smile to Isaac Jacobs.

Sources: Mrs. Ruth Jacobs; Mrs. Avi (Shoshana) Sonenthal; Tzvi Jacobs

5

Knife in the Hollow

*I*T WAS 5:30 IN THE MORNING,   just before dawn. Faige whisked her six-month-old baby down the wooden stairs, while her husband Beryl balanced their two- and three-year-olds, one in each arm. The three older children shuffled down the wooden stairs of their three-story home. The entire Levitin clan, along with myself, piled into the family station wagon. At the time, I was a Hebrew school teacher who lived in the dorm on the third floor of the Levitin's house.

It was amazing how good-natured and pleasant the children were. After all, they had been woken up and dressed in the midst of their sleep. Three of them lay in the back of the station wagon and fell back to sleep.

They knew they were going to do a *mitzvah*, a commandment of God. Their parents were always teaching classes and feeding guests, with a spirit of genuine joy and warmth. So, for the children, being dressed in the wee hours of the morning and sleeping on the hard floor of a station wagon was simply part of the joy of doing a mitzvah.

But things don't always come easily when you do a mitzvah. And things don't always turn out as planned.

The drive from New Haven to Bridgeport, Connecticut, was uneventful. A miracle in itself, being that the car dated back to the late Sixties and often staged sit-ins and other mechanical protests. But apparently God wanted them to do this mitzvah, so He let them groove down I-95, Chassidic-style, humming Jewish melodies and reciting morning prayers.

After 45 minutes, they left the highway and began looking for Oak Street, in the section of town called "The Hollow." In the Forties and Fifties, this old part of Bridgeport was a thriving

35

immigrant neighborhood of Jews and Italians. Beryl drove in circles for about 20 minutes trying to find Oak Street. Street signs were extinct in this neighborhood. Oak trees, or trees of any sort, were an endangered species. Instead, the streets were landscaped with abandoned buildings and rubble-strewn lots. It was 1985 and all the Jews had long gone; some steadfast Italians remained in the "neighborhood" and ran auto body shops, small slaughtering houses, or returned to "The Hollow" just for their motorcycle club meetings.

Finally, a man appeared, walking on the sidewalk. It was hard to tell which direction he was going; he walked with a swaying gait. The bottle clutched in his left hand seemed to be navigating him along.

"Excuse me, sir," Rabbi Beryl Levitin called out from his window. The man looked up, or rather sideways.

"Do you know where Oak Street is?"

"Right there. Just swing around by Columbus School," he said, pointing his bottle to the old grammar school at the next corner. He swung his arm around to the left, and almost lost his balance. As he straightened up, he stared at the rabbi's gentle face.

"Thank you. God bless you," Rabbi Levitin said with sincerity.

"I grad-ju-ated from Columbus," the man added, touching his chest.

The corner had a street sign pole, but the sign was gone. In the middle of the block, they saw a decrepit building, with a rotting wooden sign: *Live Poultry.*

They parked and walked into the building. Stacked crates of chickens lined the walls. Feathers, straw and chicken droppings matted the concrete floor. It was definitely a live poultry house.

"Get out the way," a voice barked. They jumped back. A gruff-looking man barged past with a crate of cackling chickens in each hand. "Can't you see you're in the way? Get by the door."

He wasn't in a good mood, and seeing Jews obviously didn't make him happy. Sweat, mixed with dirt, covered his face and his bare, muscular arms.

"I'm Levitin. We came from New Haven," Rabbi Levitin said softly, but undeterred.

"You said you'd be here by 6," the man said his eyes glaring.

Rabbi Levitin glanced at his watch: it was five after 7.

"I'm too busy. Don't have time for this nonsense," he said. He grabbed a chicken with his left hand, slapped the chicken firmly on the table, and followed through with the big butcher knife which he held in his right hand. With his left hand, the butcher stuffed the jerking headless body down a hole in a wooden plank; with the shiny blade of his knife, he swept the chicken head into a barrel off the end of the wooden table. Before anyone's stomach could make a full loop, a new chicken was in his hand, beheaded and draining.

"We'll wait till you take a break in your work," Rabbi Levitin said quietly.

"Forget it! I've got a lot of work to do. A man has to work for a living. Go home. Do your rituals somewhere else," he said with venom. He grabbed the drained chickens and stuffed them into a metal box. He locked the box, flicked a switch, and a roaring vacuum sucked the feathers through an exhaust pipe.

The man turned his back and went about his business.

Figuring there was no talking to this guy, I turned to Rabbi Levitin and said, "Beryl, should we leave?"

"We'll wait," Beryl answered.

Beryl never gave up easily when doing a mitzvah. Of course, they didn't even have to come here. On *erev Yom Kippur*, the day preceding the evening when Yom Kippur commences, it is customary to rise early and perform the rite of *kaporas*—atonement. If it is not possible to do this rite early that morning, the rite may be performed the previous day... which is exactly what many people did in New Haven at the Hebrew Day School, where Rabbi Levitin and I both taught. In the afternoon, some live chickens were brought to the school and, according to custom, the teachers swung the cackling chickens over their young students' heads while everyone repeated the verses of atonement.

But doing *kaporas* in the middle of the afternoon was too easy for Rabbi Beryl Levitin. Beryl was raised in a home in Soviet Russia, where his father worked as a kosher butcher—a job that was illegal in Stalin's days. But Beryl's father was a devoted follower of the *Frierdiker* ("previous") Lubavitcher Rebbe. So driving to Bridgeport early in the morning was certainly not called "impossible" or "difficult," especially compared to Siberia, where Beryl's father spent his final years for the Soviet crime of helping Jews eat kosher.

Likewise, waiting for that cranky butcher to give them some live chickens was not even perceived by Beryl as a test of faith. After all, everything is *hashgachah protis*, Divinely guided to the minutest detail. Persevering to do such a beautiful mitzvah on the eve of Yom Kippur was definitely something God wanted them to do. As for me, my stomach ached for some breakfast and my feet were tired of standing—after all, we had been huddled in that corner for more than an hour.

"Okay, take a chicken!" the butcher suddenly growled.

Finally. Thank God!

"My wife and daughters need hens, and my sons and my friend and I need roosters," Beryl said with a soft smile.

"What's this nonsense! I'll give you one rooster and one hen. That's enough," he said.

"One for everybody. I'm paying you for them," Beryl reminded him firmly. "White ones, please." Although it is preferable to procure white fowl, because white represents purity, it is only a *hiddur*, an extra measure to enhance the mitzvah. The butcher's hot blood rushed to his head, his face turned crimson.

"We pushed him too far," I thought to myself, praying.

He grabbed a crate and swung it through the air... onto the table.

"Hens. Take what you want," he said.

Wasting no time, Rabbi Levitin and Mrs. Levitin each took a hen and helped two of their daughters do the *kaporas*.

Chaya Elke, aged five, timidly put her little fingers onto her mother's hands which were holding onto the base of the hen's wings. The hen remained calm and quiet.

"Repeat after me," her mother said. *Squawck*, the hen screamed and wildly flapped her wings. Chaya Elke jumped back but her mother held tightly. Mrs. Levitin smiled. "Don't worry. It just makes a lot of noise. It won't bite you."

Chaya Elke held the back of the hen and repeated in Hebrew the words: "Children of man who sit in darkness and the shadow of death... If there be for a person, even one interceding angel out of a thousand accusers, to speak of his uprightness on his behalf, then God will be gracious to him and say: Redeem him from going down to the grave; I have found atonement for him."

Next step, Chaya Elke lifted the hen over her head, and while slowly turning the hen three times around her head, she repeated the following words: "This is my exchange, this is my substitute, this is my atonement. This chicken shall go to its death and I shall proceed to a life, good and long, and to peace."

Chanalah, who was three and a half, said the words with her father, as he helped her circle the hen over her head. "*Zeh kaporasi*, this is my atonement..." Chanalah repeated carefully, her innocent face shining with excitement from doing the mitzvah.

Suddenly, painful cries pierced the air. Everyone looked up. Tears were streaming down the butcher's face. He was sobbing. "What's wrong?" Beryl asked compassionately.

"My, my *Zaide* ..." choked the butcher, "my Zaide used to do that with me when I was a little boy."

Tears gushed down the butcher's face. I was shocked. I had no idea that the butcher was Jewish. Beryl softly patted the butcher's back.

"When Zaide died—I was only seven—that was the end of anything Jewish for me. My parents were too busy working; they ran a store, six days a week. Even on Sunday, they were busy, doing the books. Zaide always said his Sarahle, that's my mother, married a *goy* [a non-Jew]. Dad was Jewish, but he was a socialist. He didn't believe in religion.

"Two weeks before I turned 13 my father took me to the local rabbi and said I needed a *bar mitzvah*. The rabbi said, 'No problem. Just give me $20, he can just repeat the blessings after me. In three Sundays will be *Rosh Chodesh*, the beginning of the new month. We'll be reading the *Torah* on that day. Bring him then, at 8 A.M.'

"Like your three-year-old did just now, I repeated the words after the Rabbi. Only I was so embarrassed, being thirteen years and not being able to read on my own. I wanted my Zaide to be proud of me, but I felt I let him down. What's worse—I was saying the blessings and no one was listening. The dozen or so old men in *shul* [synagogue] were just talking and laughing throughout the whole thing. I swore to myself that I'd never step foot in a shul again. And I haven't."

"Would you like to *shlug kaporas?*" Beryl softly asked.

The Jew reached for a white rooster and repeated the *kaporas* service after Beryl, word for word. This time, no one was laughing. There were only tears.

Sources: Tzvi Jacobs, who was the teacher; Rabbi Beryl Levitin; and a Bridgeport Public Library reference librarian (for the history of "The Hollow").

❧ 6 ❧

Saying Mazal Tov is Not Enough

O N SEPTEMBER 4, 1988, I went to Crown Heights looking for a small miracle. Like thousands of other people, I came to see the *Lubavitcher Rebbe*. I took a place at the end of a long line, which meandered from the steps of the Rebbe's home all the way to the end of the block.

Waiting to see the Rebbe usually provokes a serious, introspective mood. However, the atmosphere that Sunday afternoon seemed exceptionally happy and gregarious. The beautiful summer weather certainly helped. A brilliant blue graced the sky, the midday sun shone brightly and a soft breeze fanned away the late summer heat.

It seemed to me that God was happy with the world. After all, we were still in the month of Elul, the month preceding Rosh Hashanah, when it is said that the "King [God] is in the field, and He is accessible to all the common folk in a warm, friendly manner..."

A black limousine pulled up in front of the Rebbe's house. Five distinguished-looking men stepped out and were immediately escorted into the Rebbe's home. I overheard that the men were some political dignitaries, who were seeking the Rebbe's advice.

The line stopped moving. After 45 minutes, the line resumed inching forward. I glanced behind me. The line had swelled to thousands of people, enough to prompt the police to close off the entire block to traffic.

While waiting, I read Psalms and inspected my deeds and character. Even though the Rebbe constantly demanded that we, his followers, do more good deeds, learn more Torah, and refine

41

our character, he also taught us to recognize our station in life and not to be too hard on ourselves (and especially on others) for being imperfect.

A clean-shaven man stood behind me and we began chatting. It turned out that he was an English professor at a university in Indiana and his interest in stories of the *Baal Shem Tov* had brought him to Crown Heights many times during the past 12 years.

"I came to pay my respects to the Rebbe," the professor said.

The Rebbe's wife, *Rebbetzin Chaya Mushka*, of blessed memory, had passed away seven months earlier. During the year of mourning, the Rebbe worked at his home. We kept talking until we found ourselves on the brick walkway in front of the Rebbe's house.

"These streets are paved with miracles," the professor said. He adjusted the English cap on his head. "If you ask me, the Rebbe makes miracles faster than I can flip red ink onto my students' papers."

We stepped across the threshold into the Rebbe's home. My heart was knocking hard against my ribs. Again, I tried to focus inwardly, reviewing my deeds from the recent past. Overwhelmed with my human frailties, my mind wandered off to the external features of the Rebbe's Tudor-style home: the crystal chandelier hanging above me in the front room, the high ceilings, the old but attractive lamps and chairs pushed off to the side. These well-cared furnishings were probably purchased in the late 1940s when the Rebbe and Rebbetzin had bought their home.

Everyone had entered the house single file but somehow, once inside, the line of people thickened. The professor and I nodded "good-bye" as the crowd pushed us apart. I stood on my tip-toes to see the Rebbe.

In the adjacent middle room, the Rebbe stood, leaning his left forearm on the velvet-covered *bimah:* on the sloping surface of this raised table lay a stack of fresh dollar bills. The Rebbe had already been standing and seeing people for nearly five hours, saying a brief blessing to each person and handing each one a dollar bill for charity.

Thousands of people were still waiting outside the Rebbe's home, so the line monitors were moving the line past the Rebbe as fast as they could. "Next... next... next...." A steady stream jostled past the Rebbe. The thought of merely greeting so many people made me dizzy. But one look at the Rebbe and one could see how, in that brief moment, the Rebbe gave his full attention to his visitor, as if only he and his visitor were alone together.

Suddenly, it was my turn.

"*Bracha v'hatzlacha* (blessing and success)," said the Rebbe in a low voice while handing me a dollar.

I reached for the dollar and, as soon as my fingers grasped it, a line monitor tugged on my sleeve to pull me along. I resisted and blurted out nervously, "Blessing for baby."

My wife and I had been trying to conceive for two years with no success.

Looking at me, the Rebbe said with a clear, strong voice, "Amen. In a good and auspicious time." Then the Rebbe handed me a second dollar. With every blessing, the Rebbe generally gives a dollar. The reason is because something spiritual like a blessing is more effective when it is "grounded" to something physical, like a dollar. It's like saying "I love you" and then giving a hug.

Six weeks later, my wife Esther and I were visiting Crown Heights for *Shabbos*. Esther hardly ate any of our hostess's delicious food. The nauseousness and "flu-like" fatigue lingered for a month. Finally, Esther became suspicious and went to the doctor.

"Positive," the nurse wrote on a piece of paper. Esther was pregnant. Our hearts leapt ecstaticly. The doctor performed a series of routine tests and estimated that my wife was due in six months.

Three days later the nurse called. "Mrs. Jacobs, the results of the test came back, and the fetal protein is high. We would like to schedule you for an amniocentesis."

Neither Esther nor I had ever heard of "fetal protein." I called the doctor's office to get more information.

"If the amniocentesis confirms the test results, then what?" I asked.

"We would recommend an abortion," the nurse answered.

"That's what I thought," I said, already feeling upset. "I already checked with a rabbi. Jewish law forbids an abortion under such a situation. So there's no sense in even doing the amniocentesis. In fact, you should have never even done the test in the first place."

A week later a genetic counselor left a message on our answering machine. She wanted my wife and I to come in for a consultation. I called her and asked, "If there is a problem, G-d forbid, could anything be done to correct it?"

"No, I'm afraid not," she said. "We would recommend that the pregnancy be terminated."

I took a deep breath and tried to sound calm. "What is high fetal protein indicative of?" I asked.

"Down's syndrome," she answered.

Down's?! The blood left my head and I sank down on the chair. "Bye," I said faintly, as I laid down the phone receiver. A friend of mine just had a Down's baby. His wife was having a very difficult time coping. No, I couldn't tell Esther. She had assumed that high fetal protein was something relatively minor, like low iron.

The following evening we drove to Crown Heights for a friend's wedding, and found a parking space around the corner from the Rebbe's home. Esther opened the car door.

"Esti, wait. I have to tell you..." I said. I broke down and told her. We both sat in the car, crying.

The Crown Heights siren sounded: it meant that the Rebbe was about to give a public discourse. Afterwards, he had the custom of allowing people to walk by him, and he would give them a brief blessing and a dollar. We ran around the corner to the Rebbe's home and were among the first in line: Esther in the women's line, I in the men's line.

As I waited in line, I tried to believe the Chassidic teaching that everything was for the best; this test, however, seemed too much for us.

Saying Mazal Tov is Not Enough

As I walked past the Rebbe, he said his customary blessing, "Blessing and success," and handed me a dollar. My tear-stained eyes looked up at the Rebbe, but my words were caught in my throat. I would have to write a letter to the Rebbe to tell him about the test results. I took the dollar and moved along. The line weaved out through the narrow kitchen, past the ancient two-slice toaster, and out the back door of his house. Esther was already waiting for me in the car.

"The Rebbe said 'Mazal tov' to me!" Esther exclaimed. "How did he know I'm pregnant?"

"I don't know. We haven't told anybody," I said. We were silent for a while. "The Rebbe actually said 'mazal tov'?"

"I was starting to doubt that I heard him right," Esther responded. "Then, as I was getting back into the car, I saw this magazine lying on the back seat."

The magazine's back cover was headlined, "Saying Mazal Tov Is Not Enough," with a picture below of a pregnant woman. The advertisement explained that a pregnant woman should have a card called *Shir Hamaalos*, the Psalm of Ascents, in the delivery room, as protection against any harm to the mother or the newborn baby. The custom originated in the mystical teachings of the *Kabbalah* and recently had been popularized by the Lubavitcher Rebbe.

"Where did this magazine come from?" Esther asked.

I turned it over and looked at the front cover. "Oh, I picked it up in *yeshiva* this afternoon." I looked up at my wife and said, "Esti, everything is going to be all right."

The Rebbe saying "mazal tov" was a tremendous kindness; it calmed us down a lot. On "Mother's Day," Sunday, May 9, Esther went into labor. Having been warned by friends not to panic and go to the hospital too early, we waited as long as we could before leaving the house. At 20 past midnight we drove to the Morristown hospital. Esther hobbled down the long hall, stopping every 45 seconds when the heavy contractions kicked in. She gripped the shiny hallway bars, breathed and hooted like the birthing instructor had taught her, and bent down and around until the pain subsided.

We finally made it to the maternity ward. "I think she's ready to give birth," I said excitedly to a nurse.

"We'll be with you soon. Just have a seat," the nurse said.

It was half past midnight and the nurses were having a busy night with a bumper crop of deliveries. After five minutes, I went back to the nurse's station.

"The contractions are every 30 seconds," I said anxiously. "I think you better look at her now."

A few minutes later, the nurse nonchalantly took Esther into an examination room to check her. I slid the envelope which had the *Shir Hamaalos* card inside under Esti's pillow.

"Bring the cart!" the nurse screamed.

Another contraction kicked in. "Don't push, dear," the nurse said to my wife. "Don't push. We have to wait for the doctor."

"Bring the cart in here. There's no time to take her into the delivery room," the nurse said to the other nurse with the set-up cart.

In my sweaty palm, I clutched an extra *Shir Hamaalos* card for the baby's bassinet. I stood just outside the delivery room door, anxiously reading Psalms.

"Breathe, dear. Hoot, hoot, hoot," I heard a nurse say loudly to Esther, trying to be heard over Esther's painful groans.

"Don't push. The doctor's on her way."

Esther gave another push, and the nurses made a commotion.

Two minutes later, at 12:55 am, the nurse called out, "Congratulations! It's a girl—a beautiful baby girl."

Tears rolled down my face. "Oh, God, I hope that means she's healthy."

Just then, the doctor arrived. She examined Esther and said, "The baby looks healthy." We were so excited to have a healthy baby that Esti and I stayed up until dawn, cooing over the baby and discussing names. I took an early train to Brooklyn and prayed the morning service in 770, the Rebbe's synagogue. At the Torah reading, I officially named our baby "Chaya Mushka Bracha," after the Rebbe's wife, Rebbetzin Chaya Mushka, of blessed memory.

Postscript: Esther was exceptionally happy and thankful to be a mother to a healthy, adorable baby. Two months after giving birth, she wrote a thank-you note to the Rebbe. Chaya Mushka Bracha was growing nicely with beautiful brown curls and a precocious smile. While signing the letter to the Rebbe, Esther saw a neighbor, a close friend, walk past our apartment window. She was childless and had a condition which made it difficult for her to conceive, so Esther added a "P.S." at the end of her letter: "May the Rebbe please give Leah *bas* [the daughter of] Sara a blessing to have a baby."

Three months later Esther's friend Leah said to her, "I must tell you a secret. I'm pregnant!"

A week later, Esther found out she was also expecting. We were shocked and surprised that Esther had conceived so soon after giving birth. But then we remembered the saying in the *Talmud:* "When you pray for someone else, God gives you the blessing first."

Sure enough, our second daughter was born five days before Leah's son. Since then, we have been blessed with two more daughters, thank God. Next time, I think I'll pray that a friend be blessed with a son!

Sources: Esther Jacobs; Ruth Botenaro, R.N.

∽ 7 ∽
Bound Behind the Bank

I T WAS JUST BEFORE NOON, September 1, 1989. I was driving through a seedy section of downtown Elizabeth, New Jersey, and spotted a branch of my bank.

I parked in the deserted lot behind the bank, walked around to the front entrance, and then remembered that I left my check in my car. I trotted back, unlocked the car door, and while leaning inside, fumbled through an assortment of papers and bills which filled my coat pocket. I found the envelope with my precious monthly stipend. I had already spent most of it, having mailed out a slew of checks the day before to pay some long- overdue bills. I laid my coat back over the seat, straightened up, and turned to close the car door.

"Ugh!" I gasped.

Three men had formed a tight semi-circle around me. They wore tattered jeans, filthy tee-shirts and reeked of alcohol. The man on my left was clutching the skinny neck of an empty whiskey bottle, bottom aimed upward. It looked as if he was going to hammer something... or someone. His dark, glassy eyes revealed a mean, desperate gaze. The scrawny guy on my right looked almost friendly, but a little scared and hungry. But the one in the middle—he was "Lerch," straight out of *The Addams Family*. His large, rectangular head loomed above me.

"Got some change?" Lerch asked, extending his huge hand towards the Adam's apple bobbing up and down my thin neck. My bulging eyes stared down at the maze of lines in his palm and slowly read their way up his extended arm. A skull with crossed bones, a dancing girl, and a variety of other tattoos depicting scenes of decadence and humor, adorned his long, bare arm. At the top of his arm, the ragged edges of a torn sleeve accentuated his broad shoulder. I nervously tilted my head back and lifted my eyes over his protruding chin. A deep scar had formed a trench from his chin to just below his left eye. Lerch grinned. His smile was missing at least three teeth. "Like a couple of dollars," said the guy with the empty bottle. "We're *real* hungry."

Rules of urban survival that I had recently read in a *Reader's Digest* raced through my head. "Never take out your wallet when a stranger asks for change." These guys probably saw me walking back from the bank. If they see that my wallet is empty, they might really get upset.

Another rule: "Stay calm." I took a deep breath. Why is this happening to me? Okay, everything happens for a reason. All is for the good. Only fear God. All the Chassidic dictums about life were racing through my mind. They made sense in *yeshiva* where I had been learning for the past year. "Stay calm," I repeated to myself. After all, today is *Rosh Chodesh Elul*, the first day of the month *Elul*. Elul is an auspicious month, the last month of the Jewish year, when God is supposed to be very accessible to everyone. As the Chassidic masters explain, like the king who leaves his palace and travels through the streets and fields, God makes Himself more accessible and graciously listens to the requests of ordinary people.

Oh, God, please be with me now. I have a wife and a three-month-old baby. My hands were hiding behind my back, clutching the envelope, and holding the nearly shut car door.

"Yes, I have some change for you," I said, while subtly dropping the envelope back into the car, and locking the door behind me.

Everything happens for a reason—that I firmly believed. Every single Friday, as part of the yeshiva schedule, I would visit Jewish patients in Morristown Memorial Hospital. I looked at these men. Who says I have to go to the hospital to visit the sick? I knew it was next to impossible, but maybe...

"Are any of you Jewish?" I asked, rather meekly.

"Yeah. I'm Jewish," Lerch said.

"You're Jewish?" I said, in disbelief. It must be a ploy. "You have a Jewish name?"

Pulling his head high with pride, like a foot soldier responding to his commanding officer, Lerch said, "Shmuel Yankel *ben* Moshe," declaring his Jewish name, the son of Moshe. In his eyes, I probably looked like a rabbi, with my black hat and long, untrimmed beard.

"Did you have a *bar mitzvah?*" I asked.

"Uh huh."

"You had a bar mitzvah? Where?"

"In Asbury Park. Rabbi Carlebach bar mitzvahed me."

"Wow, you *are* Jewish!"

"Of course, I'm Jewish. *Boruch atoh ahdo– elokeinu melech ha'olam...*"

Lerch—or should I say Shmuel Yankel—was chanting the blessing for the *Haftorah* which he had recited for his bar mitzvah maybe 20 years earlier. The short, wiry man slapped the whiskey bottle against his palm. I trembled. I had better try to appease him.

"Hey, why are you asking for change?" I asked. "You should be asking for millions. Today is exactly one month before *Rosh Hashanah*, the Jewish New Year, and you can ask God for as much as you want. Because a month before Rosh Hashanah, God leaves his palace and comes down in the streets with the people, and we can ask Him for anything now. As a matter of fact, God is feeling gracious towards us now. I've got a little change in my pocket—I'm just a student at a rabbinical seminary—but God, why He has billions."

As I spoke, I slipped the car key out of my back pocket. Keeping my right hand behind me, I unlocked the car door and reached for a bag on the car seat.

"Shmuel Yankel, do you know what these are?" I asked, as I unzipped a black velvet bag and took out two small boxes. He vigorously nodded, with his big toothless smile, as if I were showing him some delectable candy.

"Are you right-handed?" I asked, quickly unwrapping the leather straps from around the *tefillin* box. "Good, now put out your left arm." I slid the open loop of the hand tefillin over his large fist, up his bare arm, past the chorus line of tattoos and—what's this? A patch of little holes, at the top of the forearm, near the inside of the elbow.

"Oh, my God," I thought, "those must be needle tracks. He's really fallen low."

I slipped my *yarmulke* from beneath my hat. "Here, Shmuel Yankel, let me put this on your head so you can say the blessing with me." He leaned over so I could reach the top of his head.

"Now, repeat after me. *Boruch…*"

I said each word of the blessing and he repeated after me. Then I tightened the knot around his upper arm, and wrapped the tefillin strap around his arm, trying my best to cover with the leather tefillin straps some of the unclothed figures. As I wound the leather strap around his forearm, I explained that the hand tefillin is bound around the upper arm, next to the heart, to show that our actions must be heartfelt and bound to God.

"Now, Shmuel Yankel, lower your head, and I'll put the other box of tefillin on your head. The head is above the heart, to teach us that our head must rule and direct the desires of the heart.

"Okay, hold out your hand again." I wrapped the strap of the "hand tefillin" around the ring finger. "This shows we are married to God. Our head, heart, and actions must all be united with God."

The guy with the bottle had been pacing back and forth on the asphalt, like a hammerhead shark swimming in front of his prey." Let's do something already," the Shark finally snapped.

"You just wait," Shmuel Yankel snapped back. "Can't you see I'm prayin'!"

The Shark backed off like a guppy. He dropped his bottle on the asphalt and kicked it into the weeds.

I gulped. "Before a Jew can pray to God, Who considers every single Jew his child, we must accept upon ourselves the commandment to love our fellow Jew. We say the following words: 'Behold, I accept upon myself the positive commandment: You shall love your fellow man as yourself.' Now, cover your eyes with your right hand, like this, and we'll say the *Shema* prayer. *Shema Yisroel Ado-nai Elo-heynu Ado-nai Echad* ['Hear O Israel, the L-rd is our God, the L-rd is One']."

Shmuel Yankel wiped his eyes with his hand. They were wet with tears.

"God is right here with you, Shmuel Yankel," I said, with a choked voice. "Ask Him whatever your heart desires."

Shmuel Yankel was silent, but I could almost hear his heart sobbing. A tear rolled down from his eye into the deep scar along his cheek.

"I used to go to synagogue all the time," Shmuel Yankel said. "I liked going. But after my bar mitzvah, my parents got divorced and I didn't go anymore."

During this entire parking lot ceremony, the long-haired guy stood quietly, motionless. He looked mesmerized. Why?

"What's your name?" I asked.

"Mike," he said with a slurred French accent. "My friends call me Mike. But my real name is Michel."

"Michel, are you Jewish?" I knew that it was highly unlikely, but he had that longing look in his eyes.

"No, I'm Catholic," he said. "I don't really practice it anymore."

"It's okay whatever you are. God created everybody, and made everyone unique."

"My mother," Michel said, hesitatingly, "my mother told me she was born Jewish. When she was a little girl, the Nazis killed her parents and some nuns took her into their monastery and raised her. So she became Catholic."

"Michel, you're Jewish!" I exclaimed. "If your mother was born Jewish, then you're Jewish. Nothing can take that away. Once a Jew, always a Jew. It's ingrained in the soul. Put these on and we'll celebrate your bar mitzvah."

I was more nervous than Michel. Placing my yarmulke on his head, I said, "Repeat after me. *Boruch…*"

"Bah rook," he said, with a shaky voice. It was obvious that he had never uttered the guttural Hebrew *ch* sound in his life. I excitedly put the tefillin on his arm and head. The black box sat on his stringy black hair. His dark eyes twinkled and Michel looked like a long-lost prince who had been dragged through the mucky alleys of medieval Europe, beaten and abused, and now had finally stumbled back to the gates of his royal home, crying out to his father, the king. The king came out to the street, and Michel ran and hugged his loving father.

Michel repeated the words of the *Shema* and stood silently, with his eyes closed, for an endless minute.

"We can take them off now," I finally whispered.

Like a helpless baby, Michel held out his arm and let me unwrap them.

I couldn't believe what was happening. The King must really be in the "field." Turning to the third guy, the shark-turned-guppy, I asked, "And what's your name?"

"Joe," he blurted out. His hands were trembling.

Joe had safely positioned himself about six feet away, in front of the hood of my old Ford Galaxy. I was still standing by my car door.

"Is your mother Jewish?"

"No! She's Catholic. My grandmother was Catholic. And I'm Catholic. And I'm not putting those things on."

"Don't worry, Joe. You don't have to, you aren't supposed to," I said, showing him that I was putting them back in their bag. "A Gentile doesn't have to do this commandment. But non-Jews get a share in the World to Come, just like a Jew does, if they follow the seven commandments that God commanded them."

I then explained the *Seven Noahide Laws*, stuttering a little when I stated the prohibition against stealing. "The only catch is that a person has to observe these laws not because they make sense, and not because he's afraid he might get caught, but because God commanded them to mankind, through Moses the Lawgiver."

Joe listened silently, with no visible response.

"Hey, let's celebrate Michel's bar mitzvah," I said, breaking the silence. "I have some cake in the car."

I split the cake with Shmuel Yankel, Michel and Joe.

"*L'chaim.* To life," I said, raising my cake.

I told Michel what a great day it was for him, and how fortunate he was to have put on tefillin for the first time in his life. My two Jewish friends thanked me for the bar mitzvah, and we all shook hands and said good-bye.

"Wait, here's some change," I said, coming after them.

But Shmuel Yankel raised his arm, strong and high, stopping me in my tracks. "Thanks, but we're okay. We're okay."

Source: Tzvi Jacobs

⪻ 8 ⪼
Grandpa's Tears

"When we were young," Karen's mother said to her daughter, "your Grandpa would tell a joke: 'Do you know what a rebbe is? A rebbe is a miracle maker. He would go outside, look up at the moon, and say, 'Moon, stop shining. No, I changed my mind, keep shining.' And all of the Chassidim would say, 'A miracle. A miracle.'"

THE PHONE RANG. "Hi, Karen, it's Tzippi. We haven't seen you in a long time. Would you like to spend this coming *Shabbos* with us?"

Karen felt touched that someone from the Lubavitch community in St. Paul still remembered her. She had met Tzippi the previous summer while studying at Rabbi Manis Friedman's Bais Chana Seminary, and had enjoyed many Shabbos meals with Tzippi, her husband, and their fun-loving children.

"Thanks, I'd like to," Karen answered, "but I already have plans."

Karen had arranged to attend a weekend retreat in the country with some of her college friends. But as the week progressed, the only ride Karen could find to the retreat was leaving late Friday afternoon and would arrive after dark, after the onset of Shabbos. Although Karen had become ambivalent about observing many Jewish laws, she was not ready to break the prohibition of riding in a car on Shabbos.

By Thursday evening, Karen said to herself, "Okay, I'll give Shabbos one last chance." She called Tzippi and accepted her invitation, resigning herself to waiting until after Shabbos ended on Saturday night to join her friends at the retreat.

Karen felt good to be back in the Lubavitch community, experiencing the joy of Shabbos. Just after Shabbos concluded, Tzippi said, "Karen, a special rabbi from Chicago is coming to speak at the Chabad House tonight. Rabbi Feller has been trying for ten years to get him to come here. You really should stay and hear him."

Tzippi talked Karen into waiting until the following morning to go the the retreat. On Saturday night, February 3, 1979, a crowd of 80 people filled the Chabad House to hear Rabbi Shlomo Zalman Hecht. Rabbi Hecht was an emissary sent by the *Frierdiker* Lubavitcher Rebbe [the "previous" or sixth Lubavitcher Rebbe, Rabbi Yoseph Yitzchak Shneersohn] in the 1940s to strengthen the Jewish community in Chicago.

Karen sat at a front row table. The deep lines etched into Rabbi Hecht's face revealed to Karen that his years in Chicago had not been easy.

"It's a pleasure to see a roomful of so many committed people," Rabbi Hecht said, his face beaming. "When Rabbi Feller came here fifteen years ago, this place was void of *Yiddishkeit* [traditional Jewish life]. Now look at it!"

To Karen's surprise, the voice of the white-bearded, prematurely aged Rabbi emanated a young and vibrant spirit.

"I had the *z'chus* [merit] to be by the Rebbe on the last *Yud-Bais Tammuz* before he passed away. [The gathering on the 12th day of the month of Tammuz marked the Frierdiker Rebbe's birthday and the anniversary of his being totally freed from a Soviet death sentence.] It was then that he told a very interesting thing about the Baal Shem Tov, founder of the Chassidism. He said that the Baal Shem Tov had a custom of asking anyone who came to him, '*Vaas gedenkst du?* What do you remember?' Meaning, what event in your life sticks out in your memory?

"When the person told him what he remembered, the Baal Shem Tov explained the meaning to him as it related to that individual's own personal life.

"One of the basic interpretations of Divine supervision is that each and every individual hears that which is important for him to hear and sees that which is necessary for him to see.

"This teaching is based on a fundamental principle of Chassidic philosophy, that each and every individual has his or her unique mission in life. God puts each person in situations that he needs to experience in order to teach him what he needs to know to fulfill his particular mission. The Baal Shem Tov was interested in every person and found it important to reveal to them the significance of their experiences."

Rabbi Hecht went on to tell various stories relating to the Previous Rebbe. Karen was inspired by the stories and felt fortunate to know these Lubavitchers. But, of course, she was not one of them. As her mother had recently told her, "Papa was very religious but he was not a *Chassid.*"

Suddenly, Rabbi Hecht's deep voice boomed like thunder, jolting Karen from her reverie.

"During the war years, in Chicago," Rabbi Hecht said, "we had a fund called *Keren Hatzalah.* By the war's end, we had collected $180,000 to be distributed to the Jewish refugees in Paris and Palestine. Amongst the three people sent to distribute it was Shmuel Broida—I don't know if you know the Best Kosher Food Products; Shmuel Broida was the president and he was also the president of Keren Hatzalah."

Karen was stunned. "He's talking about Grandpa," she realized, astonished.

Rabbi Hecht continued talking. "When they came back [to Chicago, after distributing the funds in Paris], Mr. Broida gave a report and said, 'I had an experience that I shall never forget.'

"And we thought, what kind of experience can be so earthshaking? We put our ears closer....

"So Mr. Broida continued, 'In Paris there were a thousand Russian Jewish refugees. I was very interested in finding out how these people lived through all the years that they were in Russia, so I spoke to the elders, the middle-aged, and then picked at random a little boy and I asked: 'Look, little boy, I am going back to America. Is there anything that I can give you that you want very, very much?'

"And then, as tears welled in his eyes, Reb Broida said, 'Do you know what this little boy said: 'I want the *z'chus*, the merit, to come to America to see the Lubavitcher Rebbe.'

"Mr. Broida said, 'This... I can never forget.' He said he could understand an older person wanting to see the Rebbe, but a little boy of eight years old! Mr. Broida said, 'I thought he would want candy, he would want a toy, a suit, a hat, shoes. Only one thing he wanted to have: the merit of coming to America to see the [previous] Lubavitcher Rebbe.'"

Rabbi Hecht lowered his voice and said, "And Mr. Broida was not a Chassid, which was also known. So we asked Mr. Broida what does this mean?

"Mr. Broida answered us, 'If the Rebbe can leave such an impression 20 years after he has left the country, that even little children will grow up with the hope that some day they will be able to see the Rebbe—then this is something the world has not yet known.'"

"I shall never forget," Rabbi Hecht reminisced, seeming to change the subject, "when I once came to the Rebbe for *yechidus*—you know, when you meet privately with the Rebbe. In the course of the meeting, the Rebbe told me something that I didn't think had any connection to me, but at the time it occurred to me that maybe the purpose of it would become clear to me in the future. Perhaps he was entrusting me with a message for others, in another place and time. Then the Rebbe said to me, 'God fulfills every thought I have for a good thing, some earlier, some later, but God fulfills and grants all my thoughts.'"

Rabbi Hecht paused and said, "Do you know what this means? Only a man who is *kadosh elyon*, only a man who is so near to God, can utter these words."

Rabbi Hecht glanced around the silent room. Some people were wiping their eyes. He saw in the front row a young woman with tears streaming down her face.

Rabbi Feller also saw Karen sobbing. After the talk, he whispered to Rabbi Hecht that he thinks the teary young woman is the granddaughter of Mr. Broida. Rabbi Hecht approached Karen privately and confirmed Rabbi Feller's guess.

"Your grandfather and I were not close friends. He was much older than I, and well, let's just say, we had different viewpoints on certain subjects. Still we worked together on some projects. After he told the Keren Hatzalah committee about his experience in Paris, he called me and asked if I would arrange for him a private meeting with the Rebbe. It was 1947 and the Frierdiker Rebbe was in very poor health, so it was very hard to get an appointment with the Rebbe. Nevertheless, I was able to arrange it.

"We flew to New York together. After a relatively long meeting, your grandfather walked out of the Rebbe's room and said, 'This was one of the most incredible experiences in my life.' That's all he would tell me.

"Just then," Rabbi Hecht continued, "the Rebbe's secretary came out and said, 'The Rebbe wants to see you.'"

"The Rebbe said to me: 'Reb Shmuel Broida was just by me, and I asked him what he was involved in, and he told me. And then I asked, *'Vos tuen eure kinder?* (What's doing with your children?)' and Reb Shmuel burst into tears.'"

Rabbi Hecht looked solemnly at Karen and said, "I didn't understand what caused your zaide [grandfather] to cry, but then the Rebbe looked at me, and said, 'I promised him that one day he will have *nachas* [joy] from his *einikloch* [grandchildren].'"

"Until this moment, I also didn't understand why the Rebbe called me into his office and told me what he said to your Zaide."

Karen understood. Grandpa had six children and all of them stopped being observant during their teen years. When Mr. Shmuel Broida passed away, of his 17 grandchildren, not one was the least bit orthodox.

Rabbi Hecht smiled softly and said to Karen, "It was your grandfather's tears by the Rebbe that brought you back to *Yiddishkeit.*"

That night Karen decided to follow Rabbi Friedman's advice to study full-time at Machon Chana Yeshiva in Crown Heights.

Today, twenty years later, Karen and both her brothers, Michael and Chuck, are observant Jews. Karen (now known by her

Jewish name, Shifra Chana) lives a happy, Chassidic-Jewish life with her husband and children in Morristown, New Jersey.

Sources: Shifra Chana (Karen) Hendrie; Ellen Hawley, Karen's mother; and, Mrs. Yoseph Hecht, daughter-in-law of Rabbi Shlomo Zalman Hecht, of blessed memory; and an audio tape of Rabbi Hecht's talk.

❧ 9 ❧
Match Made in Heaven

"CHAIM, YOU LOOK TERRIBLE!" Shira said. Chaim's face was pale. Beads of perspiration lined his forehead, even though a large ceiling fan cooled the store.

"I have a terrible pain right here," Chaim said, reaching around to a spot on his lower back. "Since April I've been getting them. But never this bad."

Shira often shopped in Chaim's cosmetics store, which was in Petach Tikvah, a town near Tel Aviv, Israel. Being a nurse, Shira felt his forehead and checked his pulse.

"Oh, my goodness!" she gasped. "We have to get you to a hospital. Let's go now. I'll drive you."

"I'll go later. After work," he said, clenching his jaws.

That evening the pain in Chaim's back worsened. He finally took Shira's advice. Chaim's fiance, Orly, drove him to the hospital.

After a thorough exam and testing, the doctor said, "Chaim, I'm sorry, but it's too late. Both your kidneys are gone. A viral infection, coupled with high blood pressure, has destroyed them."

Chaim was shocked. He had always taken good care of himself. He exercised regularly, didn't smoke, and rarely drank alcohol. How could this have happened to a healthy 38-year-old man? Chaim felt as if his world had ended.

After staying a week in the hospital, Chaim was put on kidney dialysis. He came to the hospital three times a week to be hooked up to the dialysis machine. His blood flowed through the machine, which cleaned and filtered the blood, and then channeled it back into his arteries.

"This is not life," Chaim said to Orly. "I feel like a prisoner to this machine." Chaim stopped working and started losing money. Life had lost all meaning. He contemplated suicide.

One evening, Orly realized that Chaim was seriously depressed. Chaim had always lived up to his name, which in Hebrew means "life." But now he had no desire to do anything.

"We're going to get you a new kidney," Orly said. "Then life will be good again."

"*B'seder, ain davar* (it's okay, it's nothing)," Chaim winked at Orly, trying to act like his old "macho" self. Orly set up an appointment for Chaim to see a kidney transplant specialist.

"Chaim," said Dr. Shapiro, "your HLA tissue type is rare. You need a kidney that comes close to matching it. To be truthful, it won't be easy to find one."

Orly offered one of her kidneys, but it did not match. Chaim's sister, stepfather, and other relatives also were tested, but no matches were found.

Month after month passed, and no matching kidney was found in Israel's donor pool. In the meantime, Orly looked for other solutions. She read books, studied the latest research, talked to doctors and patients.

Eventually, her efforts paid off. She found a professor who was doing experimental research on potential kidney transplant patients. Professor Reznick would circulate the patient's blood through a machine which would remove the antibodies in the blood. Antibodies attack foreign cells in the body and can cause a body to reject an imperfectly-matching kidney. Only a donor kidney from an identical twin would be a perfect match.

Chaim and another kidney patient began thrice weekly treatments. Chaim's hope was slowly building up. After three months on this experimental treatment, the two patients were informed that one kidney was available at Hadassah Hospital in Jerusalem. The doctors chose Chaim's buddy, Raffi, to receive the kidney. His HLA tissue matched the donor kidney better than Chaim's.

Raffi's body accepted the kidney. The experiment was a success! Orly was elated, because Chaim was next on the list.

"Science has done such amazing wonders," Chaim said to Orly. "In the 1940s, Palestine was a malaria-infested wasteland and our people transformed it into an oasis. If man puts his mind to something, he can move mountains. Man makes miracles. Man is the creator of his destiny."

The experimental treatment had removed the antibodies that would have attacked the transplanted kidney. But it also eliminated the antibodies that fought infections. Two days after the operation, Raffi caught an infection. Three days later, the infection overwhelmed his body and he died. Chaim too felt like dying.

The doctors advised Chaim to stop the experimental treatment and, because of his rare tissue type, to search outside of Israel for a kidney.

For eight months, Orly wrote letters and made phone calls to medical centers throughout Europe. Finally, a center in France agreed to accept Chaim as a transplant candidate. Orly flew to Paris to sign all the prerequisite papers and make arrangements for Chaim.

"*Quel domage* (such a pity)," a bureaucrat of the French government told Orly. "Because Israel doesn't contribute a large amount of organs to the international transplant pool, we cannot give an Israeli a kidney with such a rare tissue type."

Orly returned to Israel. She looked at her notebook and saw that she had been searching for a matching kidney for two and a half years. Orly had used up her vacation time to go to Paris. She returned to work, looking depressed.

"My spirit is broken," Orly confided to Chaya, an Orthodox co-worker at the office where she worked in Tel Aviv. "I worked so hard to find a center in Europe to accept Chaim as a transplant candidate. And, look, it was all in vain."

"Orly, please go to the Orachim seminar," Chaya pleaded. "It will be good for both of you." Over the past two years, Chaya had approached Orly at least a dozen times about attending one of Orachim's periodic seminars on Jewish values. Each time Orly and Chaim said they didn't need religion to help them live.

"Orachim will be having a seminar in Jerusalem this weekend," Chaya said. "You must go. It will lift your spirits."

"Okay, okay. I'll speak to Chaim," Orly said.

Chaim and Orly went to the weekend program. They parked their car nearby. If they found it boring, they would leave and drive around Jerusalem to visit the pubs. At the registration desk, Chaim told one of the organizers, "You should know, we don't take this stuff seriously."

After the weekend, Chaya came to visit Orly at her home. "Not only did we stay," Orly said, "but we sat there Thursday night until Sunday evening, glued to our seats. We found it fascinating!"

"The lecturers prove to you that the Torah is the authentic word of G÷d," Chaim interjected. "About 50 people came to the seminar, most of them highly educated. They asked hard questions trying to stump the rabbi, thinking they could not be answered. But each time the rabbis [leading the seminar] answered them."

Chaya smiled and Chaim continued breathlessly. "The rabbis gave persuasive answers to every question asked. Scientific, historical, linguistic—the evidence was so logical. Like the accurate prediction in the Bible about Abraham's two sons: Ishmael will become the father of a multitude of mighty, warring nations—the Arab nations; and, Isaac will become the father of a small, holy nation which will inherit and conquer the Land of Israel, go into exile, and eventually return to their homeland. It's such a clear example, yet I never had taken the time to think about it.

"Then they showed us in the ancient book of *Zohar* where the diameter of the sun is recorded. But the highlight was all these amazing codes hidden in the words of the Bible. These Bible codes were discovered and 'cracked' with the use of state-of-the-art computers. At the end of the weekend, the rabbi said, 'If you believe it, do it.'"

Orly was smiling. "It opened my eyes and made me think," she said softly. "I'm not convinced that the Torah is the word of God, but one thing is for sure: after attending the seminar, Chaim has so much more life."

On the Wednesday after the seminar, Orly received a phone call from Sarah, a lady she had met at the Orachim weekend.

"Orly, I made an appointment for you to meet with Rabbi Yair Israeli," Sarah said. "His organization helps people who cannot get medical treatment in Israel find treatment elsewhere."

On the following Monday, Orly and Chaim went to Tel Aviv and met with Rabbi Israeli. After hearing their story, Rabbi Israeli advised Chaim to move to the United States, to Charleston, South Carolina. "In Charleston there is a medical school which has an excellent kidney transplant center."

"I have never heard of this town," Chaim protested. "I should go to a strange city, where I have no family, no friends? I don't even speak the language."

"I can speak English," Orly said. "We'll go together. It's our only hope left in the world."

Their hope quickly gave way to more stress as they realized what lay ahead of them if they moved to America. Orly and Chaim calculated their anticipated expenses. Chaim sold his house and personal belongings. The economy in Israel was depressed and Chaim had to sell his business at a loss. Still, they needed more, and raised money from family and friends. Orly and Chaim would soon be leaving everything, going half-way around the world, seeking a second chance at life. They had nothing but each other.

In August 1990, with only the stars above them, Chaim and Orly did what other Jews have done for hundreds of years: they were married under a *chuppah*, a Jewish marriage canopy. A month after the wedding, with all their worldly belongings in their hands, Chaim and Orly boarded a plane to the United States.

The night before *Yom Kippur*, in Charleston, South Carolina, the telephone rang in the home of Barry and Shoshana Goodman.

"Hello, Shoshana. It's Rabbi Radinsky. There's an Israeli coming to Charleston for a kidney transplant. Could you make your home available to him and his wife during the holidays?"

"When are they coming?" Shoshana asked.

"In about 20 minutes," the Rabbi answered.

Shoshana and her husband readily accepted to do the *mitzvah* [good deed]. "Nothing like running to do a mitzvah!" Barry said to Shoshana, with a laugh.

It was not the first time Barry and Shoshana knew people who needed kidney transplants. Their doctor's secretary had waited five years for a kidney. When she finally got a transplant, her body rejected it. She has been waiting five years for another kidney…and her tissue type was not nearly as rare as Chaim's!

Barry also thought of a dear friend, Rabbi Shimon C., of blessed memory. Rabbi C. waited many years for a kidney and never got one. So, with all his heart, Barry prayed that Yom Kippur for his new friend.

Immediately after Yom Kippur, Chaim started his thrice-weekly dialysis at the Medical University of South Carolina, and met with Shirley, a transplant coordinator at the University's Kidney Clinic.

"We like to find a fairly good match," said Shirley, "but thanks to a new drug, cyclosporine, the whole field of organ transplantation has been revolutionized. We can now transplant organs which have many more mismatching sites. Not only that, the survival rate of transplant patients has almost doubled."

"I've never heard of this drug," Orly said.

"It's commonly known by its trade name, Sandimmune®. It's fairly new, approved in the United States in 1983. Interestingly enough, this compound was isolated from a rare fungus growing in the soil. It's what we call a 'miracle drug'—it suppresses only those specific sites in the immune system which would normally cause the body to reject a mismatched donor organ."

"So it won't shut down the entire immune system?" Orly asked.

"Not at all. Only selected sites," the nurse said. "That's what makes it a miracle drug!"

"And my husband can use any kidney?"

"Yes, theoretically," Shirley answered. "Still, the better the match, the better the chance of survival. Chaim, with your rare tissue type, we cannot say how long it will take to find a suitable kidney. Maybe nine months to a year, maybe longer.

"In the meantime," Shirley continued, "we will give you a pager to wear at all times. When we find a matching kidney, we'll have to operate right away. We'll page you to come immediately to the hospital."

Chaim shook his head at the thought of waiting so long. Shirley then explained the charges for the dialysis and the transplantation. It was much, much higher than they had originally calculated.

There were only three days left until the holiday of *Sukkos*. Barry built a *sukkah* booth in his backyard. On Sunday the weather was lovely. In addition to Chaim and Orly, Shoshana and Barry invited two other couples to join them in their sukkah for the daytime meal. Barry recited *kiddush* over a cup of wine [a blessing to sanctify a holiday meal] and everyone sat down to enjoy a delicious holiday meal. But Shoshana noticed a worried look on Orly's face.

"Orly, can you come into the kitchen with me? I need a hand," said Shoshana.

Orly walked with Shoshana into the house. Shoshana led Orly into her bedroom and seated her on a chair. "What's bothering you, Orly? You look sad and worried."

Orly broke into tears. "There is no way I can stay in America. I'm going back to Israel."

"Why? You've made so many good friends here."

"You have been the best friend," Orly said, sobbing. "On Friday, we met with the nurse and she gave us the full price of the whole transplant. It will cost three times as much as we have. It's impossible."

Her struggle of three years, giving up everything to be in a faraway place to find a matching kidney for her husband, seemed hopelessly lost.

"Everything will be alright, Orly," Shoshana said. "God has brought you and Chaim to Charleston for a purpose. You are only being tested by God. Don't worry. We'll raise the money."

The two women returned to the sukkah, and Shoshana explained the problem to the others.

"My father-in-law is always finding ways to help people in need," Nava said. "I'll call him and tell him about Chaim's situation."

"Don't worry, Orly. You and Chaim are like family. We'll help raise the funds," Lynn said.

Times were financially tight in Charleston. Shoshana had no idea where she would find such a large sum of money, but several of her friends from the Jewish community met together and they agreed to raise the remainder of the money.

Chaim and Orly were raised in secular homes in Israel, where Jewish customs and observance were not a part of their lives. Ironically, in Charleston, they became immersed in a traditional Jewish world. Other Jewish families were inviting Chaim and Orly for Shabbos meals and to other activities. They studied Torah with the rabbis in town, and became regular Shabbos worshippers at the "Minyan House," a small house which served as the neighborhood's Orthodox synagogue. Chaim also started coming to the weekday morning services, and Rabbi Radinsky gave Chaim a pair of *tefillin* [prayer boxes] to wear during prayer.

On Shabbos, Orly also prayed at the Minyan House, and enjoyed the lively services and the warm hospitality. Still, Orly did not share Chaim's commitment. "I believe in God," she told a friend, "but I'm not ready to accept all the Orthodox do's and don'ts."

Orly and Chaim moved into an apartment in Barry and Shoshana's neighborhood. Transfusions were costing Chaim $860 a week. Month after month passed with no word of a matching kidney, and medical bills were rapidly depleting the couple's savings. The Charleston Jewish Federation stepped in and subsidized their rent, food and some of their medical bills.

Chaim tried to earn money by fishing in the rivers which surround the peninsula of Charleston. He borrowed a small fishing boat, went out into the Ashley River, and a fish almost bit his pole in half. It turned out to be a shark!

After that experience, Chaim decided to stick to dry land and do some gardening work. Feeling very grateful to the Charleston

Jewish community, he planted a beautiful flower garden in front of the Minyan House. Of course, the amount of physical activity he could do was very limited.

Orly and Chaim celebrated Chanukah, Purim and Passover, but still no kidney. A matching kidney could come up at any minute of the day or night, and Orly always carried the pager with her. With each passing day, the risks rose. At this stage of kidney failure, the body simply could not operate like a normal, healthy system. The chance of a heart attack or some other organ failure was very high.

They had been living in Charleston for eight months. One day the pager went off. Orly's heart jumped. They have found a kidney! She called the hospital to tell them Chaim was on his way.

"Sorry, it was a mistake," a nurse said. "Someone had dialed the wrong pager number."

Orly felt like giving up and going home. "Who knows if they'll ever find a kidney?" she cried.

In June, the Charleston *Post-Courier* newspaper interviewed and photographed the Israeli couple. "To wait is very hard," Chaim told the reporter in his broken English. "The life stops. Last year I would have given up. What gives me strength today is my belief in God… to believe that nothing happens by accident, that God writes the show. We only have to trust the Director and act our best."

On the first Shabbos in July, Orly and Chaim ate the Friday night meal with Barry and Shoshana. At the meal, Chaim said, "If I'm blessed with a new kidney, God willing, when people ask me what happened to me when I was in America—I will tell them: 'Number one, I got Torah, and number two, I got a kidney.'"

Three days later, on July 7 at 7 am, the pager went off again. The hospital called their house and told Orly that a kidney had been found for Chaim and to bring him in right away. Orly immediately drove to the synagogue where Chaim was praying the morning service.

"Chaim, hurry. Take off the *tefillin*. The kidney is in!" she whispered in an excited voice.

"It will wait until I finish *davening* [praying]," Chaim calmly said. During the next ten minutes, Chaim finished his prayers and carefully wrapped up his *tefillin*. He felt a profound awe and trust in God.

They drove the three blocks to the hospital. After seven long hours, Dr. Charles Fitts came out of the operating room and said to Orly, "Mrs. Micha, the operation went exceptionally well. We were able to attach the blood vessels with no complications. You should expect your husband to stay hospitalized for at least ten days, while we monitor him for rejection episodes and infections. The next two weeks will be critical, but so far, everything looks good."

While the doctor spoke, tears streamed down Orly's face. She tried to say "thank you," but she couldn't get the words out.

Twice daily, a nurse injected Chaim with Sandimmune® to try to prevent the transplanted organ from being rejected. Still rejection of the new organ could occur.

Ten days after the operation, Dr. Raja Rajagopalan took a biopsy, a sample of tissue from Chaim's new kidney. He examined the tissue for cell destruction, a telltale sign that the kidney is slowly, but surely, being rejected by the body.

While waiting for the doctor to return with the results of the biopsy, Orly and Chaim were discussing their dreams for their future... if all went well. "God willing, when we get back to Israel, I'm going to pray at the *Kotel* [the remaining wall of the Holy Temple in Jerusalem] and thank God for giving me a new life, and ask Him to give Barry and Shoshana a baby."

Shoshana was already in her late thirties and had been trying for many years to have a child.

Looking into Orly's eyes, Chaim added, "And then I am going to pray that we are also blessed with a child."

With a clipboard in his hand, Dr. Raja tapped on Chaim's door and entered the room. "Mr. Micha, we'll have to monitor you closely for the next two months, but the results, so far, look good... very good. There are no signs of rejection."

Match Made in Heaven

Orly and Chaim with their baby daughter

Two months later, in September, the nephrologist gave Chaim a clean bill of health.

"My kidney's good?" Chaim asked.

"Yes, you can leave. Chaim, you can go back home," the nephrologist said with a big smile.

The Charleston community gave Chaim and Orly a warm, teary-eyed, good-bye party, and the couple flew home. In Israel, Chaim quickly regained his strength and started a business delivering fresh eggs to stores and restaurants. Along with the eggs, Chaim told everyone how he found more than just a kidney in South Carolina. He inspired many of his customers to become more connected to Torah and mitzvahs.

Orly wrote a letter in July 1994 to a friend in Charleston: "We are very happy to be home. Both Chaim and I have become *shomer Shabbat* [Sabbath observant] and are studying Torah and attending seminars and classes. We are expecting our first child."

From the Heavens to the Heart

In September 1994, Orly and Chaim had a baby daughter and named her "Cheyn," Hebrew for 'grace;' in December, their friends, Shoshana and Barry, also had their first baby, Avraham Aharon Moshe. Who knows, those two babies might some day also be a perfect match... for marriage!

Sources: Chaim and Orly Micha; Barry and Shoshana "Goodman;" Dr. Charles Fitts and Dr. Raja Rajagopalan of Medical University of South Carolina, Charleston, S.C.; Dr. Mark Grebenau of Novartis Pharmaceuticals Corporation, maker of Sandimmune® and Neoral® "miracle" drugs.

৵ 10 ৵
Light Up the Darkness

THE FLAMES DANCED BACK AND FORTH and swirled around, their light reflecting in the crystals of the Tiffany chandelier which dazzled above. With a will of their own, her fingers slowly peeled back the final piece of tape. With the gift-wrapping paper spread apart, she lifted the cover of the box and gently reached inside.

"Oh, they're gorgeous!" Jill exclaimed. "They are the most beautiful slippers!" With a quick leap she was on her feet, twirling around on the tips of her toes. Happily, she kissed her grandmother and grandfather.

"Happy Chanukah, Jilly, my lovely ballerina," said Grandma, with a hug. "*Kayn ein hara* [no evil eye], you're growing up so fast." Glancing at her husband, Grandma sighed, "Before you know it, she'll be a *kallah* [bride]."

Jill blushed.

"Just remember," Poppy said, looking sternly into her eyes. "One day you'll make your own Jewish home. You must marry a Jewish man. You'll have *kinderlach*. That's real *nachas*. Nothing else will bring you true happiness. Don't ever forget it!"

How could Jill ever forget it. Every time she saw her grandfather, that's what he would say. Like a broken record, he would explain over and over again that by marrying a Jewish man and raising Jewish children, she would keep Judaism alive. She and her husband would be sharing their heritage together. Any other marriage just could not work.

Jill ran upstairs to her mother's old bedroom and locked the door. "Why can't Poppy leave me alone!" She fell on the bed and cried.

Even though Jill was only 12, she felt that her grandfather's argument did not ring true. She had friends whose parents were both Jewish, and their marriages ended in divorce. She also had friends who had only one Jewish parent, and their marriages looked good. His narrow view of the world just didn't make sense to her. Even Jill's parents taught her that all people should be judged on their merits, and not on superficialities like race or religion.

High school years came. Still Jill would not see how she could ever reconcile her secular lifestyle with her religious grandfather's rules. "How can you watch that garbage! Don't you know it fills your mind with *narishkeit* [nonsense]?" he would say every time he saw Jill and her siblings watching television. Poppy rarely watched anything and, then, of course, it had to be educational. Jill could not figure out her Poppy. Granted, he was a founding member of a synagogue in Long Island, went to services with his wife every Friday night, and afterwards went home and made *kiddush* at the Friday night meal. But Poppy was not a fully observant "religious Jew;" he was a modern, successful businessman. So where were all these archaic ideas coming from?

Wasn't seeing two of his three daughters marry Gentiles enough to teach him that he was fighting a losing battle? It was certainly enough to break his heart.

But the pain seemed only to make him more adamant.

Jill loved her Poppy, but she could not believe in the dictums he preached to her. At age 18, she began her first year at the University of Massachusetts at Amherst. Among the regular courses, she signed up for a course in Judaic Studies. She wanted to decide for herself what place Judaism would hold in her life. The course description sounded open-minded, not archaic.

The Judaic Studies course exposed her to more modern viewpoints which confirmed her beliefs that Poppy's ideas were not the final word. Jill's first semester whirled by and she delved into her new world. On the last Saturday night of the semester, practically everyone stayed in the dorm, cramming for final exams… and suddenly Jill remembered: "It's the last night of Chanukah. I didn't do anything." Her family always went to her grandparents and celebrated Chanukah. She thought about her approaching exams, and sadly sighed, "Chanukah just passed me by."

A block away, Rabbi Chaim Adelman was winding down from a week full of Chanukah activities. The Sabbath had just ended at the Chabad House, and Rabbi Adelman was perusing a fax he received on Friday afternoon, minutes before *Shabbos*. "This is unusual," Rabbi Adelman said to his wife. "I can't remember the Rebbe ever saying a *sicha* [a talk] so close to *Shabbos*. The Rebbe spoke about the importance of spreading the message of Chanukah."

Rabbi Adelman felt his Chanukah programs were successful. The turnout at the Chanukah party was certainly much greater than the previous year.

Beeep. Another fax was coming through the machine. It was also issued from Lubavitch Headquarters. Apparently, just after *Shabbos* concluded, the Rebbe spoke about the urgency of "lighting up the darkness of the world" by doing Chanukah outreach on the last night of Chanukah.

Now, Rabbi Adelman knew he must do more. And he knew exactly what he must do: real outreach work, without waiting for the students to reach out to him. He had to go to where the students were. But how?

John Adams, a high-rise dormitory, loomed almost above his Chabad House, just a block away. The only student he knew in JA Dorm was Marty, but he had gone away for the weekend. How could he get into the dorm? Rabbi Adelman had not yet been issued an official campus chaplain identification badge.

When a house is on fire, there's no time for formalities… especially when the Rebbe makes an urgent request to fight the fires of assimilation.

"Tom. Hi, this is Rabbi Adelman. I know Marty's away, so I wonder if you could do me a big favor?"

"Sure, Rabbi. What is it?"

"Tonight is the last night of Chanukah and I need to give out *menorahs* to the Jewish students in JA. Could I say I'm visiting you to get past security?"

"Hey, no problem. You're cool, Rabbi."

Rabbi Adelman filled up a large shopping bag, rushed to the dorm, passed security, took the elevator to the top floor, and knocked on the first door. One roommate was Jewish. Rabbi Adelman gave him a menorah and candles, and the student happily lit it. He proceeded from room to room giving out menorahs to the Jewish students, and snapping pictures of each one lighting the candles. He wanted pictures for his Chabad House scrapbook, as well as some to send to the Rebbe.

Rabbi Adelman was so well-received that he ran out of menorahs. He ran back to the Chabad House, refilled his bag and continued working his way down the 22-floor dorm. At 11 pm he reached the 17th floor.

A minute later, Jill heard someone knocking on the doors down the hall. Then she heard a knock next door.

"Hi, it's Chanukah. Are you either of you Jewish?" the confident, warm voice asked.

"No, but the girls next door are."

Jill was already opening the door as the Rabbi's hand reached out to knock. "I would love to light Chanukah candles," Jill said. Excitedly, Jill placed the golden-colored menorah on the sill of her window, and began setting in it eight colored candles. The sky outside was very dark.

"Our job is to light up the darkness of the world with the light of Torah and mitzvahs," said Rabbi Adelman. "This is the meaning of the Chanukah lights."

Jill said the blessings and lit the candles. She was so thrilled. Just like when she was a little girl, she watched the candles dance away the darkness.

During the entire visit, her roommate Melanie was on the phone shaking her head. Rabbi Adelman snapped a picture and left. Melanie got off the phone. "How did he get into the building? How do you know he's really a rabbi? Who knows! He can't be a rabbi. Chanukah's over already. And he told you to light after dark. You aren't allowed to light candles after dark," she said, confusing the strict rule of lighting Shabbos candles

Lighting the Chanukah menorah

before sunset on Friday with that of the Chanukah candles, which are meant to be lit at night. Melanie became more and more frantic, and Jill became confused and upset.

Jill called her mother in Long Island and told her what happened.

Rabbi Adelman continued on his way through the dorm, giving out more menorahs, going from floor to floor. He trotted down the stairwell going to the third floor, the metal menorahs clanking in the bag.

"Stop!" barked a voice from behind. "Drop the bag and raise your hands in the air."

A second man flashed his badge in Rabbi Adelman's face.

"Campus police. Put your hands on the wall."

They frisked him rather roughly. "Let's see some identification."

Rabbi Adelman was still dressed in his Shabbos clothes, and having walked from the Chabad House to the dorm, he didn't even have a driver's license on him. "I'm the rabbi from the Chabad House, and I was giving out these Chanukah menorahs to the Jewish students."

It was already midnight; they ordered him out of the dorm. "And don't speak to anyone on your way out," one officer said in a nasty tone.

The Rebbe had urged everyone to do their utmost, and Rabbi Adelman knew he had carried out the Rebbe's request as far as he could.

The next day, the Chabad House phone rang. "Are you the man who was in JA Dorm last night with the Chanukah things?" a young woman asked. Her voice sounded very distraught.

"Yes," he answered, trying to connect the voice with one of the many coeds he met that night.

"Who are you? Why do you do this?" she asked.

"I have a Chabad House on campus. My job is to reach out to the Jewish students, educate them about their Jewish heritage, and give them the opportunity to do mitzvahs, such as lighting the Chanukah menorah or enjoying a Shabbos meal."

The girl still sounded distraught; she asked more questions and then, convinced that he was a real rabbi, said "Bye."

Life went on and Jill buried the incident in her memory. But constantly popping into her consciousness were his words, "Our job is to light up the darkness."

Jill majored in dance therapy, and learned how to help people heal their troubled spirits through the medium of dance.

In the spring of her junior year, Poppy passed away. His three daughters could never see his view of reality. They saw a world in which God did not care if a person ate shrimp, cheeseburgers, or other unkosher foods. Nor could they see an intrinsic difference between a Jew and a Gentile. So Poppy fought a tough battle. Too tough. Of his three daughters, only Jill's mother married a Jewish man.

Jill was the oldest daughter, the second-born of five children. Which way would she go? After Poppy's death, it seemed as if he exhorted her from the grave, "Marry Jewish. Keep Judaism alive." The question kept popping up in her mind. It would not die with Poppy.

September of her senior year, Jill went to Israel on a quest to understand her Jewish identity. She enrolled in Hebrew University in Jerusalem, and took the traditional Jewish studies program. Among other courses, she signed up for Jewish mysticism, taught by a *Chabadnik*, a Lubavitcher, named Rabbi Baruch Kaplan. Jill asked many profound questions about God and the Jewish soul.

"If a soul is spiritual, how can orthodox law say it is passed through the mother, and not the father?"

"First, let's understand what a soul is," Rabbi Kaplan said.

The question took many classes to answer. Jill took advantage of other Jewish classes offered throughout Jerusalem, and dropped in for classes at different yeshivas. Every week she accepted another family's invitation to spend Shabbos, and she asked more and more questions. Until one day Jill woke up and realized that she was seeing the world totally differently. She felt as if she had been living her whole life in a dream, and now felt as if she was waking up for the first time.

Jill went through a trying time in Israel, struggling to find her way. She would often sit and pray by the *Kotel*, the "wall"— the only wall of the destroyed Holy Temple which miraculously could not be knocked down by the enemies and remains standing to this day.

"Please God, if only I could meet a wise old rabbi who would be able to look into my soul and know everything about me, and could comfort the pains in my troubled soul," she cried.

The first semester at Hebrew University was coming to an end. Chanukah menorahs lit up the narrow streets of Jerusalem. On the eighth night of Chanukah, Jill went to the Kotel. There was a huge crowd. "What's going on?" she asked in Hebrew to a young woman.

"The Rebbe of Lubavitch is going to be there, on the giant video screen," she said. "By satellite hookup. We'll see live scenes of Chanukah celebrations from around the world: the Rebbe's synagogue in Crown Heights, Eiffel Tower in Paris, Red Square in Moscow, Australia."

Chabadniks and others poured into the Kotel area for the "Chanukah Live" celebration. The rain also poured.

Fraught with the excitement of seeing "The Rebbe," Jill stood in the rain, her clothes sopping wet, to get at least a glance of this man. Finally, she saw the Rebbe on the huge screen. His eyes focused on a vision which was beyond seeing. The Rebbe gazed and Jill felt as if the Rebbe was seeing the whole world. Jill did not understand Yiddish, but his words echoed with a clarity and resoluteness that reminded her of Poppy.

Six months later, Jill left Israel and returned home to Long Island. She did not know if she was strong enough to live again in the irreligious atmosphere of a college campus.

In the middle of the summer, Jill drove with a friend to Amherst, Massachusetts. Jill knocked on the door of the Amherst campus Chabad House. No one answered. The door was unlocked, so she stepped in.

"Hello?" she called out.

"I'm downstairs in the office," Rabbi Adelman answered.

"Hi. My name is Yosefa Goldstein," Jill said, using her Jewish name. "I have work/study and I'm looking for a job for the fall semester. It will be my final semester of college."

Rabbi Adelman saw that she was articulate and poised.

"Your final semester!?! Where have been the past three years? We're always looking for help."

"I learned in Amherst my first three years, but last year I was learning in Israel at Hebrew University. I took a course in Jewish mysticism and became observant."

"Great! You got the job," Rabbi Adelman said. "I need help even before classes start, on orientation day. Can you be here August 28th?"

Jill and another student worked at the orientation table with Rabbi Adelman. During a lull between meeting new students, Jill said, "Rabbi Adelman, I have a confession to make. But you have to promise not to hold it against me."

"Shoot," said Rabbi Adelman, with a big smile.

"Do you remember about four years ago, giving out Chanukah menorahs in JA dorm?"

"Yeah," he said, slowly.

"Do you remember the call you got the next morning?" she asked.

"That was you? That was the scare of my life!" Rabbi Adelman said with utmost seriousness.

"What do you mean?" she mumbled, with a confused look on her face.

"The police. Didn't you call campus police on me?"

"No. I called no one, only my mother. I never heard anything about campus police... oh, no," she paused, and took a deep breath, "my mother must have called her friends in the New York City police department."

Jill became very close with Rabbi Adelman and his wife, and helped organize many programs for the Chabad House. That December she graduated from college and spent the first days of Chanukah with her family in Long Island. Jill tried to enlighten her family with her new view of reality. She felt the frustration that her Poppy must have endured. To say the least, it was not a happy Chanukah or a delightful *Shabbos*.

"No one sees," she cried to herself.

On Sunday, after a traumatic four-day trip into her family's reality, Jill followed through with her original plan and went to Crown Heights to attend the "Yeshivacation" program.

Jill dropped off her belongings at Machon Chana Women's Yeshiva and went to the first lecture of the ten-day program.

Rabbi Manis Friedman was speaking about the commandment of serving God with joy and avoiding sadness to the utmost.

"Sadness exists so it can be avoided, rejected. It's something to be avoided. Like when you walk into a dark room, you don't try to utilize the darkness, you simply turn on the light and the darkness is gone."

Just then, a loud siren went off. Everyone got very excited.

Jill had never been in Crown Heights and didn't know what all the commotion was about.

Someone of authority announced, "The Rebbe is having *yechidus* [private meetings]. Whoever did not have *yechidus* last night should go to 770." Whatever it was, Jill knew she didn't have it; she had never ever seen the Rebbe in person. She followed the parade as it hastily crossed Eastern Parkway.

"What's *yechidus?*" Jill asked the woman who had instructed her to come along.

"We're going to walk past the Rebbe to get a blessing," she said, a little short-winded. "Just follow me, I'll tell you in a minute."

A long line had already formed, winding onto the sidewalk in front of 770 Eastern Parkway.

The women's line had stopped moving; the men's line was now moving past the Rebbe.

"When one has a private audience with the Rebbe," her British friend said, "it's called a *yechidus.* Literally, it means 'uniting.' The Rebbe's lofty soul encompasses all the souls of the generation. His job is to unite with every person, and kindle and raise each person's inner light, to raise millions of lights. And, it is our job to carry that light to the outside, to light up the darkness."

The women's line inched forward. Finally, Jill and her friend entered 770 and stood in the cramped vestibule.

"There he is," the English woman whispered to Jill. The Rebbe sat in the doorway of his office. One by one, with hardly a gap in between, each woman stepped in front of the Rebbe, and stepped away. The Rebbe looked at each person, and moved his lips, breathing the words of a blessing.

Jill's turn came. She stepped in front of the Rebbe. The Rebbe looked at Jill/Yosefa. The moment lasted an eternity. No, for that moment, time did not exist. This was *yechidus*, a true meeting of souls, the soul of a Jewish child being revealed and united with the soul of the *tzaddik* of the generation. The Rebbe's countenance exuded warmth and happiness—and, yet, there was more. Although a massive stroke had crippled his body and left him unable to speak, the Rebbe sat like a seasoned general, confident of victory, giving every last ounce of his strength to his foot-soldiers to win the final battle.

The Rebbe gave Yosefa a silent nod. She sensed that the Rebbe was saying to her: "I know who you are and I have been expecting you. Now, keep going forward. You are on the right path."

A split second passed and Yosefa stepped away. Somehow, without words, the Rebbe answered her unasked questions. She felt that the Rebbe understood her and her troubling questions vanished.

After all, had not the Rebbe heard and answered the cry of a lost soul many years before? Four years earlier, when a freshman named Jill lit eight candles in her dorm room.

"On the eighth day," Yosefa said to herself. "Hey, today is also the eighth day of Chanukah!"

Yosefa finished the 10-day "vacation" yeshiva and began studying full-time at Machon Chana Women's Yeshiva. Two months later, she drove a carload of fellow students to Amherst. They spent Shabbos at Rabbi Adelman's Chabad House, reaching out and teaching other young "Jills." For the next two years, Yosefa studied in Machon Chana and returned once a month to Amherst to run a *Shabbos* program.

Today, living up to her Jewish name ('Yosefa' means to increase, 'Zahava' means gold), Yosefa Zahava's tiny bottle of pure oil constantly nourishes the flame in her golden menorah, burning bright with the Rebbe's teachings. Watching from above, an angel whispers, "Poppy's heavenly lamp also burns brightly, glowing with the *nachas* [joy] that his granddaughter will marry only Jewish."

Gazing at the dancing lights, Yosefa whispers back, "Thank you, Poppy. I love you, too."

Author's note: Yosefa and Yaakov Bankhalter were married June 22, 1995, and are serving as emissaries of the Rebbe, reaching out to hungry souls in the East Village of Manhattan.

Sources: Yosefa Bankhalter; Rabbi Chaim Adelman

ᴥ 11 ᴥ
Striking Oil

*A*VRAHAM ran straight to Uncle Joe's law office. By good fortune, his cousin Glen was also there.

"I need help from both of you," Avraham said, catching his breath. "I want to put up a Chanukah *menorah* on the Green!"

"Give me a call in a month or two," Uncle Joe said, without looking up from his paperwork. "Right now, we're too busy to discuss the idea."

"Chanukah, Uncle Joe," Avraham said with emphasis. "I want to put up a menorah *this* Chanukah!"

"Allan, isn't Chanukah only two weeks away?" Uncle Joe asked Avraham, his newly religious nephew who grew up with the English name 'Allan.' "Waterbury might be a small town, but things don't move that fast. We have to present our case at Town meetings, file for permits, play all kinds of politics..."

"Yeah, Cousin, let's wait till next year," Glen said. "You can't build such a structure overnight. You'll need strong supports for the branches and electrical wiring for the lights. Besides my men are in a race with winter, trying to get roofs on about a dozen houses."

"But a menorah lighting ceremony on the Green would be a fantastic grand-opening promotion for Waterbury's new Chabad House," Avraham said.

"Sorry, Allan, you have to be realistic," Glenn said.

Four months earlier, in the summer of 1985, Avraham Weisman had returned to his hometown of Waterbury, which sits quietly in the southwestern foothills of Connecticut. He had just spent two inspiring years learning at the Rabbinical College of America in Morristown, New Jersey. Now, living again in Waterbury, Avraham could no longer watch his fellow Jews

87

slowly lose their Jewish identity. He opened a Chabad House, an outreach center to teach and spread Judaism.

But it's tough fighting a battle all alone. Especially when you're 28, single, and live in a town where you're the only man who wears an untrimmed beard and a black hat.

Avraham felt more alone than the original hero of Chanukah, Judah the Maccabee—at least Judah started off with his four brothers to fight the wicked Syrian army.

Opening and running a Chabad House on a shoestring budget also didn't help him fight the battle against Jewish apathy and ignorance. But if there was one thing Avraham learned during his two years of study in yeshiva was that a Lubavitcher Chassid, a devoted follower of the Rebbe, is never alone. The Rebbe is always with him.

The Lubavitcher Rebbe would surely approve of erecting a large, outdoor Chanukah menorah. After all, public menorah lightings had been popularized by the Rebbe himself.

Every Jew is commanded to light the menorah in a place where it can be seen by others. Why? The lit menorah publicizes the miracle that happened in the Land of Israel some 2,100 years ago: The Jewish victors had found a sealed bottle of pure olive oil in the defiled Holy Temple, and the one-day supply of oil miraculously burned in the Temple's menorah for eight days. This miracle has always taken precedence over the miracle of the military victory of Judah the Maccabbee and his small band of freedom fighters against the large, mighty army of the enemy. After all, the ultimate purpose of Creation is to bring spiritual light into the world, not to simply fight evil.

That's what Waterbury needed: a giant Chanukah menorah to publicize God's miracles. But what was Avraham to do, succumb to reality and postpone a public menorah ceremony until the following year? Although in the first half of the Century, Waterbury had been a thriving Jewish community—at its peak there were 15 kosher butchers in town—now there were none. Merely getting together a daily *minyan* of ten Jews in the solitary Orthodox synagogue was a struggle. Young Jews were totally forgetting their Jewish roots. No, he could not wait another year.

Disheartened, Avraham spent the next *Shabbos* in Crown Heights, Brooklyn. On Saturday afternoon, he attended a *farbrengen*, gathering, with the Rebbe. As was his custom, the Rebbe said his scholarly discourses on the Torah in Yiddish—a language that was still foreign to Avraham. Seeing the Rebbe and being with thousands of other *Chassidim* gave Avraham strength and inspiration, but still no concrete solutions concerning the new Chabad House in Waterbury.

When *Shabbos* ended, Avraham stood on the sidewalk in front of 770, waiting for the Rebbe to step out of the building and enter his car. Avraham stood by himself on the sidewalk, at the foot of the driveway, a good 20 feet from the Rebbe's parked car. A small group of people crowded near the Rebbe's car door, and the Rebbe nodded to each of them as he entered his car.

Avraham caught a glimpse of the Rebbe as he lowered himself into the back seat of his car. Then, just before sitting down, the Rebbe raised himself back up, turned his head, and gazed across the roof of his car.

The Rebbe stared straight at Avraham. To Avraham, the gaze seemed to be forever. The Rebbe re-entered his car and the driver drove off. The other students ran over to Avraham and asked him what was going on. Avraham was speechless.

Later that night Avraham related the incident to his host. "It was one of those 'blessing stares.' The Rebbe was trying to tell me something. That I must do something."

First thing Monday morning, Avraham called the office of Waterbury Mayor Joseph Santopietro. He spoke with the Mayor's assistant and explained his idea. A half-hour later, the Mayor's assistant called back. "Rabbi Weisman, the Mayor thinks it's a wonderful idea. Let us know what we can do to help you."

Avraham rushed to Uncle Joe's law office. Coincidentally, his cousin Glen was again there working on some legal papers.

"The Mayor said we could put up the menorah on the Green! Uncle Joe, all I need is a letter formally asking for permission to put up a menorah. And, Glen, you don't have to build anything. Just please sketch me a plan on how to build the menorah," Avraham said, while handing Glen a pencil and paper.

Glen said he was really too busy, but finally gave in. Being a drafting artist and an electrical engineer, Glen drew a plan for an 18-foot high menorah, with four two-by-fours branching off from each side of the middle shaft. Large glass bowls would be mounted on top for electrical lights.

"It's remarkable, Glen," Avraham said. "Your diagram of the menorah matches the Rebbe's version how the menorah should look… the straight branches, all of them coming out of the main shaft of the menorah."

Avraham reached out for the diagram, but Glen folded it and put it in his pocket. "Al, you'll never be able to build this," Glen said, pausing just long enough for Avraham's smile to sink into his brown, bushy beard. "You better start making a bunch of Bubby's *latkes* [potato pancakes, a traditional Chanukah food]."

Two days before Chanukah, Glen and his crew erected a magnificent 18-foot high, 2,000-pound menorah.

On the first night of Chanukah, a crowd came to celebrate Waterbury's first public menorah lighting. Gary Wallen of the popular band Shlock Rock played live music, and Avraham's relatives served latkes and handed out personal menorahs and Chanukah *gelt* (coins) to the children.

Avraham felt joyful beyond words seeing all the happy faces. He knew then and there it was worth all the effort in the world to expose his Jewish brethren to the light of their heritage.

The next morning, Waterbury's Republican-American sported on its front page a full-color picture and story of the town's first Chanukah menorah. The Chabad House of Waterbury got off to a beautiful start.

Three days later, Chabad was again on the front-page of the local newspaper. The headline read: *Weisman Pulls End Run*. A well-heeled local organization accused Rabbi Avraham Weisman of sabotaging their attempt to force the Mayor to remove the Christmas decorations that have graced the Green every year for the past 100 years. They claimed that putting religious symbols on public property was contrary to the United States Constitution which mandated a separation between state and religion.

Now, Avraham understood why the Mayor was so eager to give him permission to put up the menorah. The Mayor probably figured that if the Jewish citizens were also given permission to celebrate their holiday on public property, then freedom of religion would prevail—which advanced the true intent of the Constitution. At the time of his request, Avraham did not know that the Mayor was embroiled in a behind-the-scenes legal battle to remove the Nativity scene and other holiday decorations. It was such a politically opportune time to put up a menorah.

After the story hit the headlines, an emergency Town Council meeting was called.

The attorneys of the opposing organization argued masterfully against allowing a menorah on public property. The Mayor argued for the right to display the menorah, because most Waterburians also wanted to display their religious symbols on public property. From the Mayor's perspective, the intent of the U.S. Constitution's "separation of church and state" clause was to protect freedom of religion. After some passionate discussions and closed-door political arm-twisting, eventually everyone "saw the light" or, at least, looked the other way.

Waterbury Town Council unanimously approved the menorah on the Green. The following December, the second annual Waterbury menorah lighting ceremony was a resoundng success.

After the ceremony, Avraham flew to Miami to be part of a slightly larger crowd: possibly the largest menorah lighting ceremony since the times of the original Chanukah menorah lighting in the Second Holy Temple. At Avraham's behest, the late Mr. Joe Robbie, the father of Avraham's college buddy, gladly and graciously granted permission to Chabad of Florida for a menorah lighting ceremony at the new Joe Robbie Stadium, home of the Miami Dolphins. A crowd of 70,000 football fans witnessed the lighting during the pre-game show.

Big crowds are a special treat, but putting up a new menorah each year in the small towns around Waterbury has became Avraham's Chanukah goal. In 1992, the neighboring town of Naugatuck also granted permission for a menorah on public property, after a lively, year-long battle. At the lighting ceremony in Naugatuck, a businessman from nearby Watertown asked Avraham if he would help him get approval for a menorah in his town. It has been a tough battle, but what's new? Good will overcome... eventually.

Many were sure the Chabad House of Waterbury would not last even one year, but miraculously it has lasted ten and beyond. And new "pure oil"—which is hidden deep within everyone's soul—is being discovered and refined daily.

Source: Rabbi Avrohom Weisman

~12~
Walking into Fire

*H*I, MOM. Got my orders today," David said.

"Orders for…?" she said, not finishing her sentence.

"Saudi," said David, clutching the telephone receiver. "I have to leave first thing tomorrow morning."

"Oh, no," his mother said, her "no" echoing in her 20-year old son's head.

"I was assigned to the 101st," David said with a sinking voice, as he slumped against the glass wall of the phone booth. "I almost cried when they told me."

The 101st Airborne Division, nicknamed the "Screaming Eagles," fought on the front lines during all the wars—World Wars I and II, the Korean War, Viet Nam. An endangered species, the soldiers of the 101st were trained to be fodder for the enemies: only a fraction of the early ranks had ever returned alive.

David doodled on the foggy glass of the phone booth while waiting for his mother to speak. She tried to find encouraging words for her only son, but it was hard. She had never been able to get used to her son's rebellious nature. When he was 16, he had become involved with orthodox Jews and made himself separate from the family by eating only kosher. Two years later when he joined the Army, she just about gave up. Now, upon hearing this ominous news, all she could think was "I told you so."

The Gulf War had broken out a month earlier, on January 17, 1991. David knew he would be on the front lines, facing the open jaws of the ravenous war. "They said we'll be there at least a year. I don't know when I'll see you again." David cleared his throat and added faintly, "Take care, Mom. I love you."

David closed the door of the phone booth and walked back to his barrack. Gazing at the snow-covered hills surrounding Fort

Knox Army Base, in northwestern Kentucky, he was awestruck by their quiet beauty, as if seeing them for the first time. He wondered if he would ever see them again.

As he ambled back, he thought of the preposterous story circulating around the army base that someone had predicted the war would end by Purim, the Jewish holiday which praises God for saving the Jewish people from a decree of annihilation some 2,300 years ago.

"Purim's only a month away. No way it will be over by then!" David said to himself.

Saddam Hussein certainly fit the character of Haman, the villain of the story of Purim. The wicked Haman paid off the king of Persia in exchange for a decree to command the populace to massacre all the Jews in the Persian Empire. For a full year, Haman publicized a royal edict that on the 13th day of the Jewish month of Adar, the citizens of the vast Persian Empire must rise up and kill every Jew who still clung to his faith.

Similarly, for a whole year Saddam Hussein publicized that he would "burn half of Israel" with SCUD missiles laden with deadly chemical gas. Those missiles would surely maim and kill thousands of Israelis and prove to the Arab nations that Israel was vulnerable. Then the world would clearly see that God had forsaken the Jews as the "Chosen People," and that instead Saddam Hussein had been chosen to rule the world. The scenario sounded preposterous... until Saddam Hussein invaded Kuwait.

Back at the barracks, David stood beside his cot and *davened* (prayed) the evening prayer. He was grateful for having reached his Mom, who lived with his younger sister and step-father in New Hampshire. But still he wished his Mom would accept him as an observant Jew.

David kissed his prayer book, and placed it in a small cardboard box. His personal belongings were being shipped home, while he was being shipped to war to defend Kuwait and Saudi Arabia. According to Saudi law, any Jew found within its borders would be executed. So, as a precaution, the U.S. Army had rewritten the military tags and records of David and the two other Jews in his battalion to conceal their Jewish identities. In addition, the Army ordered David not to take his prayer shawl, prayer book, or any other Jewish paraphernalia aboard the plane.

Before falling asleep, David vividly recalled news clips of the SCUD missiles fired at cities in Israel. These Soviet-made missiles stretched 40 feet long and had been enhanced with a 600-pound, European-made payload of explosives. Designed to flatten buildings, the explosion of a SCUD warhead created a frontal pressure wave. This powerful wave blasts away concrete, and sends shattered glass flying up to 1,400 feet away in all directions, creating a torrent of lethal "knives."

David felt safe in his bunk in Kentucky, but he could not help but feel pain for his fellow Jews in that narrow strip of land called the State of Israel. As he lay in his bed, he continued to recall the news he had heard and read from Israel. The first night that SCUD s were fired at Israel, one of them made a direct hit on an apartment house in a crowded Tel Aviv neighborhood. As a result of this midnight strike, 400 apartments housing 1,200 people were either destroyed or damaged. Tel Aviv hospitals were prepared to handle mass casualties, as had been the experience in Teheran, Iran, when Iraq fired SCUD s into Teheran's neighborhoods in 1988 during the Iran–Iraq War.

The ambulances arrived at a Tel Aviv hospital. One young man had some scratches from broken glass; a woman had a sprain; the injuries were all minor.

"The 'victims' could have doctored themselves," said one of the hospital staff. "Even the non-religious declared it a miracle."

During the first week of war, Iraq fired about two dozen SCUD s at Israel and damaged or destroyed thousands of apartments and other buildings. On the first Saturday of the attacks, one SCUD scored a direct hit on a bomb shelter, which was used as a makeshift synagogue on Saturday morning; two hundred worshippers were packed inside. The blast flung the people around like rag dolls. Only the shelter's eastern wall, upon which the ark housing the Torah scroll leaned against, remained standing.

When Prime Minister Yitzchak Shamir visited the site, he asked if there were any people in the bomb shelter.

"Yes," replied Tel Aviv Mayor Shlomo Lahat, "Two hundred. They were saved by a miracle." No one was injured.

How long would their *mazal* (good fortune) last? To protect Israel, David was ready to risk his life. With that thought, David whispered the *Shema Yisroel* (Hear O Israel) prayer and fell asleep.

The next morning David and more than 300 other soldiers boarded a chartered 747 towards Saudi Arabia. They refueled in Rome at midnight and took off after two hours. Within minutes, David drifted into a deep sleep. In what seemed like minutes later... a blinding light flooded the cabin of the jet.

"Oh, my gosh," David said, covering his eyes. The two other soldiers in his row were still sleeping. David squinted at the numbers on his watch. He had slept six hours. David peered through the thick window next to his seat.

"So this is Saudi," he mused. A harsh sun reflected off the whitest sand he had ever seen. Miles and miles of sand. For the next hour and a half, all David saw below was white sand, with an occasional darkened area which appeared to be some sort of man-made rock formation.

"Our guys are going to die defending this sand?!" David thought to himself. These thoughts and any other thoughts about the war were not discussed among the soldiers. Only small talk would be tossed around, or they would play cards or chess, anything to take their mind off the gruesome reality of war. Otherwise, as it had happened too many times in the past, a soldier might become severely anxious thinking about the grim future...

The 747 jet landed in the coastal city of Dhahran. David stepped down from the plane into the heat—115 degrees. He felt like he had marched into a huge solar oven. The soldiers were transported across the burning sand to a stadium-size tent. They were directed to their cots and told to go to sleep. As he lay on his cot, David wondered what the morning wake-up routine would be.

Walking into Fire

At 5:30 the next morning, nerve-shattering alarms blasted the dawn. In a heartbeat, David reached for his gas mask, took the required quick breath, and strapped the mask to his face. The maximum time limit for this procedure was 15 seconds; David did it in 3 seconds flat. Thousands of gas mask rehearsals had finally paid off.

Like a machine gun firing into the dark, David's heart pounded uncontrollably at an invisible enemy. Three minutes later, an officer came into the tent and announced, "The Iraqis fired a SCUD, and our Patriot missile intercepted it. No gas has been detected. Keep your masks on until the signal is given."

"So Saddam did the wake-up for us," David mused to himself. No gas was detected and no one was injured, but Saddam won a round on the psychological battlefield. Besides the constant fear of chemical weapons, Hussein had another silent ally: the desert. The first troops sent in August had all become sick with heat strokes. Even in the "winter," the midday temperature always rose above 110 degrees. The desert proved to be a harsh, foreign environment. Water had to be rationed. Showers were allowed only once a month.

Hussein proved himself to be more cunning and his soldiers more entrenched than originally thought. Dave was hearing reports that Hussein could drag out the war for years.

Every day, just before sunset, the hot, white sun would turn bright red, and at sunset, it would appear to melt into the sand— orange-red lava flowing off a huge ball of fire across the white sand. Then, within minutes, the temperature would drop 50 degrees. Everyone would have to wear thermal gloves and a warm jacket to keep from shivering. The temperature would be only 60 to 70 degrees, yet because of the rapid and drastic change in temperature, the soldiers would feel as if they were freezing.

In addition to his attacks on Kuwait, Saddam Hussein kept firing SCUDs into Israel. Civilian targets were hit, buildings were destroyed, but the human injuries were surprisingly light. Back in the States, many Americans were concluding that the SCUDs were basically harmless, giant firecrackers.

Then, on the morning of February 25, David and 100 other soldiers received orders to fly that evening to Al-Khobar. They would be staying in the nearby Army barrack, which had originally been a large, steel-framed warehouse. Later that evening, during suppertime in the U.S. Army barrack in Al-Khobar, Saddam Hussein's men fired a SCUD. A fragment of the SCUD blasted through the barrack's metal roof, followed by a gigantic explosion which was heard for miles around. Nothing was left of the barrack, except an eight-foot-deep crater.

The next morning an officer came into the soldiers' tent in Dharan and announced, "Last night, at 20 hundred hour (8:23 P.M.), Saddam Hussein launched a SCUD missile, hitting an Army barrack in Al-Khobar. Twenty-eight soldiers were killed in the ensuing explosion; 89 others, wounded." No one could speak upon hearing the news.

"I'm supposed to be dead," David said to himself. David and 100 fellow soldiers were scheduled to fly the previous evening to Al-Khobar and reside in that barrack. But, at the last moment, the plane had malfunctioned and could not transport the soldiers. The "malfunction" had saved their lives.

Before that attack, the American soldiers felt no anger towards the Iraqis, but now they were enraged. They wanted Saddam Hussein dead. Like Haman, the evil advisor to the king in the story of Purim, Hussein was the enemy—the embodiment of evil. And just as when the name of Haman is said during the public reading of the Scroll of Esther on the Purim holiday, everyone stamps their feet and makes noise, these soldiers felt rage toward Saddam Hussein and wanted him stamped out, once and for all.

The Gulf War intensified and the Allied forces became more aggressive, sending countless air-raids into Iraq. The Army transferred David to the front line, 50 miles from the village of Ur Kasdim, where the Jewish forefather Abraham had refused to bow down to the idols of the king. The pagan king subsequently threw young Abraham into a fiery furnace, yet miraculously he was not burnt.

98

On the quiet nights, when sorties were not taking off from the Army's makeshift runway, David often gazed at the stars. There were no lights for hundreds of miles and David could see thousands of stars in the Milky Way. Here the blessing and promise to Abraham, "I will increase your seed as the stars of the heaven" (Genesis 22:17), had great meaning.

Up to now, Saddam's army had fired more than 30 SCUDs that struck Israel. If only he could drag Israel into the war, then the other Arab nations would unite with him, and he would rule the oil-rich Middle East and the world would be at his mercy.

The Allies continued to bomb Iraq. Then, on February 27, after a mere 100 hours of Allied fighting, the BBC announced that the Persian Gulf War was over. Not for a moment did any of the soldiers believe it.

Two weeks later, on March 11, 1991, Newsweek published a cover story on the war and called the Persian Gulf War "a triumph of almost Biblical proportions." Only after returning to the United States, did David find out that the War had actually ended on Purim.

David was so happy to return home to America. When he got his box of personal belongings, he opened the box, removed his *tallis* (prayer shawl) from its bag, kissed it and hugged it, and flung it open over his head—in the middle of the Army base parking lot.

Not only did David return from the War, but every single soldier in the 101st Airborne Division—the "Fighting Eagles"— returned home, alive! Like in the days following the miracle of Purim, joyous celebrations and prayers of thanksgiving were held in towns throughout America, and "the days of darkness were converted to light, joy and happiness" (Scroll of Esther).

Thirteen months after the Gulf War ended, while stationed at Fort Campbell, David spent *Shabbos* at the home of Rabbi Zalman Posner in Nashville, Tennessee.

"David, have you seen this booklet?" Rabbi Posner asked. The booklet was entitled, "I Will Show You Wonders: Public Statements of the Lubavitcher Rebbe, Rabbi Menachem M. Schneerson, Shlita, Before and During the Gulf Crisis."

David had never before heard of the Lubavitcher Rebbe. On that *Shabbos*, he learned about the Rebbe's predictions regarding the Gulf War, how the Rebbe publicly proclaimed that the Land of Israel would be safe and that nobody in Israel would need gas masks, and that it was said in the Rebbe's name that the Gulf War would end by Purim.

Following the Gulf War, David completed a two-year stint in the Army and joined the ranks of young men learning Torah in the world-renowned Yeshiva Tiferes Bachurim at the Rabbinical College of America, in Morristown, New Jersey.

Sources: Private First-Class David Zuk; "Missiles and Miracles: The SCUD Story" by Rabbi David Rothschild, in Nefesh *Magazine, 1992; "Why Were SCUD Casualties So Low?" S. Fetter, G. Lewis and L. Gronlund, in* Nature, *Jan. 1993.*

☙13☙
A Change of Heart

"D ID YOU SEE SHIMON'S FACE?" my wife whispered as we were leaving the Grand Ballroom. "Yeah," I sighed deeply. "He looked away when he saw me."

Tovah and I walked down the marble stairs of the Crown Heights Jewish Center. "Well, it's good that we were invited to two weddings this evening," Tovah said with a smile.

"Thank God!" I said. "Let's go. I feel very uncomfortable being in the same place as Shimon."

We walked down Eastern Parkway, past 770, the Lubavitcher Rebbe's synagogue. I could hear the Rebbe's words echoing in my head, "*Hinei, hinei Moshiach ba!* [Behold, Messiah is coming]."

My wife must have felt the same words. "Yoseph," she said, "you and Shimon were good buddies. You should settle your differences."

We reached the next wedding reception and, in the festive atmosphere, I danced away any feelings of remorse. The following day, however, the troubling thoughts returned. I phoned a *Rav* [a rabbi qualified to serve as a Jewish judge], and briefly described the case. "Should I bring this case before a *Beis Din* [Jewish court of law]?" I asked.

"This case must be brought before a *zabla*," the rav said.

"A *zabla?*" I asked.

"Each side chooses a rabbi, and the two rabbis choose a third rabbi, and they all three judge the case. Call Rabbi Beryl Sherman on Chandler Street, he'll arrange it."

On Sunday morning I called Rabbi Sherman. The line was busy. I hit redial a dozen times. Finally the phone rang. "You just missed him," a young man answered.

"When can I reach him? It's very important," I said.

"Try after 4," he said, and hung up.

I called at 4:30 pm, but the line was busy. Again and again, I got the busy tone. Was God trying to tell me something? Finally, at 5, the phone rang. "May I speak with Rabbi Sherman, please?"

"Speaking."

"I need to schedule a *zabla*," I said.

"Fill out the form and mail it to me," he answered.

"Wait! Where do I get a form?"

"On the door of the *Beis Din*." Click.

I stopped at a friend's home. "Mosh, the *Beis Din* told me I have to set up some kind of *zabla*."

"A *zabla!*" Mosh said with a hearty laugh. "They try to settle the cases peacefully, but they can be quite confrontational. Too bad you can't go to Rabbi Wichnin. He was like a one-man court. He always found a way to bring both sides closer."

"So what should I do, Mosh?"

"I don't know. If you go through a *zabla*, get Rabbi Zev Pinsky. He'll represent your side well. He'll tear up any argument."

I went home with a heavy heart. How I wish I could ask Rabbi Wichnin's advice.

But that was impossible. For 18 years, Rabbi Dovid Wichnin taught the students in Yeshiva Tiferes Bachurim, in Morristown, New Jersey, and served as its Rosh Yeshiva. An outstanding Torah scholar and teacher, Rabbi Wichnin would spend precious hours every week listening to and advising students and community members who clamored for his wise counsel.

I clearly remember the last time Rabbi Wichnin sat down with the men of the Morristown Lubavitch community. It was the holiday of *Shavuos*, when we commemorate the receiving of the Torah on Mount Sinai. The skies were a sunny blue as he and his wife walked from the Rabbinical College campus to a holiday luncheon on the lawn of a congregant's home. His slow, dignified gait belied the immense effort and pain he carefully concealed. After a while, his many former students who had settled down in

Morristown gathered around their beloved teacher. Rabbi Wichnin humbly asked each of his students to express some words from the heart. It was a tender moment. We were expressing words of gratitude and affection, in case… After listening to each person, Rabbi Wichnin spoke about an issue that was on everyone's heart: unity.

That was Rabbi Wichnin; he dealt with the tough subjects—like my entanglement with Benny Bart. Years earlier, Benny's father had asked for my help with a personal problem, and Benny resented my involvement, so Benny made me his scapegoat. I don't want to go into details, but I had to swallow a lot of garbage. Many times Rabbi Wichnin and others intervened and tried to make peace, but the peace plans were accepted like annoying Band-Aids which were soon peeled off.

"Yoseph," Rabbi Wichnin eventually said, exasperated, "this probably won't get solved until Moshiach comes. In the meantime, try to avoid Benny."

Now, sitting under a stately oak, our esteemed teacher introduced the topic of unity, and then sat silently for a moment, stroking his beard. Throughout his life, Rabbi Wichnin weighed his words before speaking them. He looked around: Everyone knows about the vital importance of Jewish unity, but how does one achieve this elusive state? he asked. Everyone has a different opinion and a different perspective. And the more an issue touches one's soul, the stronger one's opinion will be.

With the deftness of a Talmudic scholar, Rabbi Wichnin built up the question, and spoke with the heartfelt sincerity that only someone who was preparing to meet his Maker could feel. Despite the seriousness of the subject, he interspersed his words with his original wit which made us all smile and laugh. He led us to see that the subject of unity was more complex and enigmatic than we had ever imagined. And then, with a moment's deliberation, Rabbi Wichnin dissolved the insurmounable walls of ice with his brilliant yet simple advice: do little acts of kindness. If you see someone needs help unloading a car, offer to help. If it's his birthday, give a gift. Many things don't even have to cost money. Even a smile or a simple hello or a compliment can warm up a cold relationship. And, of course, learning Torah with an individual or a group is the best way to promote unity.

Seven weeks later, on the 26th day of Tammuz, 5754 (July 24, 1995), Rabbi Wichnin's soul ascended to its Maker.

A full year passed. More than a thousand former students and friends of Rabbi Wichnin came from all over North America, and even from England and Israel, to commemorate together the first *yartzeit* [anniversary of the passing] of Rabbi Wichnin. The seated crowd listened to Rabbi Wichnin's eldest son complete the *Talmud* tractate he had learned in memory of his father. Then, one by one, a dozen relatives, friends, and former students approached the microphone. They recalled Rabbi Wichnin's Torah insights, his shining qualities, and his manifold roles—as a Rosh Yeshiva in Morristown, as Rav of the Tzemach Tzedek Shul in Monsey, New York, as a devoted husband and father, and on his only "morning off" from yeshiva and synagogue, as a visitor of the sick in a Monsey hospital.

In Yeshiva, Rabbi Wichnin constantly lifted our spirits with his quick wit and upbeat sense of humor, so I was shocked when I heard a close friend, who knew Rabbi Wichnin from his childhood, tell the crowd: When Rabbi Wichnin was a child of five living in White Russia, he and his family fled the invading Nazis. Starving and freezing, in southeastern Russia, the little boy helplessly watch his dear mother and sister starve to death. How did he ever overcome such a trauma—and become a wellspring of faith and hope!

Others spoke about Rabbi Wichnin's attachment and humble devotion to the Lubavitcher Rebbe and his unshakable faith in the imminent coming of *Moshiach*. The more I heard about Rabbi Wichnin, the more I realized that he lived his whole life with the belief that Moshiach could appear at any moment. "At any moment Moshiach could walk in the door or through the window," the Lubavitcher Rebbe said at the beginning of his leadership in 1951. No doubt Rabbi Wichnin yearned for Moshiach every day and was ready at every moment, but I certainly did not grow up that way.

A Change of Heart

Rabbi Dovid Wichnin

"If I truly believed in Moshiach's imminent coming, would I be acting this way?" I asked myself. "Maybe my belief is weak? But I heard the Rebbe say that Moshiach's arrival is imminent, and that these words are not just a prayer or a wish, but words of prophecy."

Towards the end of this sad yet inspiring evening, I walked to the back of the banquet hall. Shimon was leaning against a wall. I reached into my pocket and walked up to him. "Hi, Shimon," I said, with a smile.

"What's up?" Shimon asked.

I clicked my pen. "I owe you some money. Can you hold a check 'til Friday?"

Shimon smiled. "Sure."

I wrote a check and handed it to Shimon. He casually put it in his shirt pocket. "So how's everything?" Shimon asked.

"*Boruch Hashem* (thank God), the family's fine."

I drove back to Morristown feeling much more ready to face Moshiach. The points of contention went beyond the check I wrote, but a check in the pocket always warms the heart of a struggling businessman.

That was Sunday evening. On Tuesday evening, I came home from work and found a letter in my mailbox. Inside was a check for a sizable sum made out to me; no letter, just the check.

I telephoned a friend. "Yaakov, what's going on? Your return address was on an envelope; inside was a check from Benny Bart."

"Yeh, I helped him with an investment and he made good. He wanted me to share some of the profits with you—he said something about not treating you right and wanted the check to be a goodwill offering."

"Wow, Yossi, I can't believe it. Benny wants to make peace."

ᔣ14ᔣ
Shooting Straight

ALMAN STERN KNEW that as long as he had his cameras, he would be able to make a living anywhere. And that was just the way he liked it—to be independent, to be free.

In October 1971, he made a big move. He left his home in Lexington, Kentucky, and came to Crown Heights in Brooklyn to learn about his Jewish roots.

Six weeks later, the head of the Jewish seminary, or *yeshiva*, took Zalman aside and said, "From now on the yeshiva will support you. You will no longer have to pay for board or tuition. Only, give me your cameras and I will lock them in my safe. That way you will be able to learn without any distractions."

Zalman was taken aback. "If I agree," he asked, "when can I have my cameras back?"

"When Torah flows through your veins, instead of film developer," the silvery bearded rabbi replied. In 1965, at the age of 69, Rabbi Yisroel Jacobson had established *Yeshiva Hadar HaTorah*, the first yeshiva for college-aged men who had little or no background in Jewish studies.

After a long moment, Zalman said, "I will attend yeshiva full-time, but I still want to do photography on the side and pay my way."

The following Saturday night, Zalman had an appointment with a wedding photographer in Far Rockaway, a neighborhood in Queens, New York.

At 10 P.M., Zalman left the yeshiva, and walked to the end of the block, to the Kingston Avenue subway stop. There he took the Number 2 train to Manhattan. At about 11 o'clock, he transferred to the AA train for Far Rockaway. It was after midnight when he arrived at the photographer's home. The lights were out.

He rang the doorbell. Some lights switched on. "What do you want?" an irate voice rattled through the front door.

"It's Zalman Stern. We have an appointment."

"An appointment—at one o'clock in the morning?! Are you *mishuga* [crazy]!"

"I came by subway and didn't know it would take so long to get here," the young student answered. The cold winter wind blew through his thin overcoat, making him shiver.

Finally, the door opened. "Well, you're here already. Come in," the photographer grumbled.

Zalman showed him a portfolio album of pictures he had shot. "It's quite obvious that you know your stuff," the photographer said at last, "but, young man, I don't care what kind of hot-shot photographer you are, if you show up late to a wedding like you showed up at my house tonight, you'll miss shooting the bride's *Bubby* [grandmother], and then the bride's mother is going to shoot me."

It was 2 A.M. when Zalman left the house. He knew he'd never get hired. Besides, he decided that being a wedding photographer was not for him.

After a long wait at the train station, he boarded the double-A back to Manhattan. It was a local, so it stopped every few blocks. He opened the book he had brought along which included the story of Abraham, the first Jew. It told how Abraham came to believe in one God, and how God tested his faith. When the wicked tyrant Nimrod threatened, "Either worship my idols or be thrown into a fiery furnace!" Abraham replied, "I am not afraid. If God so chooses, fire will have no power to burn me." Nimrod cast Abraham into the fiery inferno. Miraculously, the fire did not burn him.

The train ride seemed endless. Zalman looked up from his book. The car was empty. He walked to the next car and the next. The whole train was empty. He had no idea where he was. All the maps in the train were covered with marker and spray paint. It was impossible to read them. At the next stop, he noticed that the ticket booth was still open. He jumped out of the subway car to ask directions. A white-bearded, black gentleman was sitting in the booth reading a Bible.

"Pardon me, sir," Zalman said, with his slight Kentucky drawl, "could you please tell me how to get to Crown Heights, Brooklyn?"

"Take the double-A to Manhattan, switch to the number 2 at 42nd Street," the attendant answered mechanically. "At this hour the double-A don't run but once an hour. You shouldn't have gotten off that train, sonny."

"Thank you," Zalman sighed with fatigue. The clock in the booth read 2:45. He sighed again and turned to head back to the platform.

"Sonny-boy! If you want, I can give you a shortcut," called out the man in the booth.

"That would be great," Zalman said. It was like a blessing from heaven.

The man sketched a map on a scrap of paper. "Go outside of the station house, through those doors," he said, pointing to the exit doors, "and take a right. At the corner of the building is a fence. Climb through the hole in the fence, and follow the path alongside the tracks. The path will go through a field."

The man pointed to a line he had made on his map. "Y'see here, at the end of this field, you'll find an old, swinging bridge hanging across the tracks. Don't mind what it looks like..."

He lifted himself off his chair and looked Zalman up and down. "It'll hold your weight. Now, on the other side of the bridge, there's a long staircase that leads into an alley. Make a right into the alley and walk 5 or 6 blocks, until you see an elevated platform for the IRT.

"Make sure you have a token," he said as he slid the hand-made map through the slot in the toll booth window. "The booth at that station closes at midnight."

"I have a token," Zalman said, reaching into his pocket to double check. "By the way, can you tell me where I am?"

"East New York," the man answered.

Zalman had no idea where East New York was, but it sounded pleasant enough. "God bless you," Zalman said, with heartfelt sincerity. The image of a swinging bridge brought back memories of his childhood in Kentucky.

He headed out of the station house, map in hand, eager to get back to his warm yeshiva dorm. His eyes teared from the cold wind. Dark clouds pushed their way across the sky. An old chain-link fence butted up against the side of the station house. Sure enough, there was a hole in the fence. Zalman crawled through.

He spotted the path. The "field" was littered with broken glass, rusty oil drums, and car fenders. Two huge rats munched on a pile of garbage. They didn't pay any attention to the slim young man quietly ambling by.

Pressing on, Zalman came to the swinging bridge. Gingerly he walked to its center, and gazed around. There were old abandoned apartment buildings all around, whose broken windows looked like dark vacant eyes. Rotting garbage lay in heaps. Graffiti covered the concrete walls. He listened for a while to the eerie silence of the empty train tracks that disappeared into the distance.

Finally, Zalman trotted down the rusty, metal stairs and stepped into a dark alley.

"Empty your pockets!" a voice growled. Zalman gasped. A .38 calibre revolver pressed against his chest.

A young man, age 24 or so, stood at the other end of the gun. *Click!* He cocked the gun's hammer. "Empty your pockets before I kill you!" He pushed the barrel of the gun harder against Zalman's chest.

"Once he finds out that I only have a subway token and small change, I'm probably done for," Zalman thought. "I'd better get ready to meet my Maker."

Suddenly, Abraham's words welled up in his heart: "I fear not for my life, for if God so chooses, the [gun]fire will have no power to burn me." Zalman gripped the book and realized that this situation must surely be a test from God. He took a slow, deep breath and prepared himself to say *Shema Yisroel*— Hear O' Israel, the Lord is our God, the Lord is One."

A sense of calm and inner strength came over him. He looked straight into the man's dark eyes and said, "Before I empty my pockets, there is something you must know: God gave everyone in the world seven basic commandments. One of those commandments is 'Thou shalt not steal.' If you steal from me, you will lose your portion in the World to Come."

Zalman decided not to mention the commandment of 'Thou shalt not murder.'

After a moment, the man frothed, "I hate Jews!"

"Why do you hate Jews?" Zalman asked.

"You see this slum," said the gunman, "this used to be the Jewish suburbs. When the blacks moved in, the Jews moved out. Soon the neighborhood became the way you see it today. Except for that apartment building." He pointed with his .38 to a high-rise in the distance. "That's the nicest building in East New York. An' it's owned by a Jew."

Zalman did not grasp his logic. Why did he hate Jews? Just then, another man emerged from the shadows, carrying a large club. "Man, what's taking so long?" the club man asked the gunman.

"This Jew is giving me jive," the gunman responded.

"Then shoot him!"

"L-let me explain," Zalman interrupted. Again, he told them about the seven commandments. "If you steal from me, you will lose Eternal Life."

The club man said angrily, "Is your God white? I don't like no white Gods like I see in the pictures."

"My God is invisible," Zalman answered. "He is the Creator of all colors. And my God is not a person. In fact, He has no form at all."

They seemed to accept his words. Zalman continued, "You know, we can make peace with each other. And if we do, and you don't steal from me, God is going to owe you. And when the time comes, He's going to pay you a big reward."

Silence. An alley cat screamed in the distance. Then, the club man turned to the gunman, and said, "He is a jiving Jew! Keep me covered and I'll empty his pockets."

"Put your hands in the air, Jew boy," the club man said.

Zalman raised his hands in the air. The club man lifted the edge of Zalman's winter coat with his club, and put his other hand into the pocket of the young man's slacks. His fingers became entangled in the strings of Zalman's *tzitzis*, so that he couldn't reach all the way into the pocket. He began to thrust his hand violently in the pocket. This caused the *tzitzis* to tighten around his fingers.

Cursing, the club man pulled out his hand, but the twisted strings held fast to his fingers. He suddenly became terrified and dropped his club. Frantically, he untangled the strings from his fingers. Free at last, he jumped behind the gunman.

"What you doing?" the gunman asked.

"This Jew's wearing pocket guards," the club man said.

"There's no such thing," the gunman responded.

"I'm telling you the truth. Some kind of strings grabbed onto my hand and wouldn't let go."

The gunman slapped his gun in his palm. "You expect me to believe that?"

"Okay. Keep me covered," said the club man, "I'll show you." Zalman kept his hands raised high in the air. The man picked up his club from the ground and used it again to lift the bottom of Zalman's coat. Then they both bent down to examine the tzitzis.

"They're not strings," said the gunman. "They're elastic bands."

"No man, they're strings," the club man insisted.

"Elastic bands!"

"Strings!"

The argument became so heated that, for a moment, Zalman thought the gunman was going to shoot the club man. Suddenly, the gunman pushed the .38 back into Zalman's chest, while the club man coiled his bat over his shoulder, as if he was going to smash his head like a cantaloupe.

The *Shema* prayer was on the tip of Zalman's tongue.

In unison they growled: "What are those things?"

They were pointing at Zalman's "strings." Slowly he lowered his hands and pulled out the *tzitzis*, lifting them up so they both could see.

"You see these knots?" Zalman said, showing them the knots made from the strings. "There are five knots... one, two, three, four, five. And coming out of these five knots are one, two, three, four, five, six, seven, eight strings. Five plus eight equals thirteen. These strings are attached to this four-cornered woolen prayer shawl which I wear under my shirt. The Bible calls these strings *tzitzis*."

They were still silent, as if spellbound by what he was saying. Zalman kept on talking. "Each letter in Hebrew equals a number, and the letters of the word *tzitzis* add up to 600. Five knots, plus eight strings, plus 600 equals 613, which is the number of Commandments God gave to the Jewish people. By wearing *tzitzis*, we are always reminded of God and His commandments."

There was a long silence. Then both men said, "Naaaaah."

"You putting us on," said the gunman.

"I'm telling you the truth," Zalman answered.

"I want to see your God. Where can I see your God?" the gunman asked.

Zalman answered, "My God fills the world. He is bigger than the world, and He is continuously creating the world. In fact, He is creating this whole scene right now."

Just then, large snowflakes floated down from the dark sky. "Now God is making it snow. And He makes each snowflake different. My God is also creating you, and if you choose to do evil..."

Zalman looked straight through both of them. He felt like Abraham standing before Nimrod. "I accept with love whatever God chooses to do with me," he proclaimed.

The club man turned and walked away, disappearing back into the darkness. The other one tucked his gun into the waist of his pants. "Where you headed?" he asked.

"I'm trying to get to the Number 2 train," Zalman said.

"Man, you going to die six times before you reach the Number 2. But don't you worry, I got this," he said, pointing to his gun.

Taking the gun in his left hand, he draped his right arm over Zalman's shoulder, and escorted him to the elevated platform.

The next day Zalman told Rabbi Jacobson what had happened. "God has many messengers," Rabbi Jacobson said in a soft voice. "Now you must *bentch gomel* at the Torah reading."

"What does that mean?"

"It means you thank God for His kindness because He saved your life."

"Rabbi Jacobson, do you still want to lock up my cameras?"

Rabbi Jacobson smiled and took the cameras. True to his word, Rabbi Jacobson supported Zalman while he studied in yeshiva for the next four years.

During that time, Rabbi Jacobson skillfully infused Torah into Zalman's veins, and taught him many secrets of Jewish mysticism, including the ancient mystical art of *Hisbonenus* (Jewish meditation).

Source: Shneur Zalman Stern, meditation teacher—last spotted wandering in Israel with camera in hand.

∽ 15 ∾
Super Neshama

I N THE SUMMER OF 1974 , 14-year-old Dave Morris travelled with an American ski and tennis camp to the Swiss Alps. Snow skiing in the summer proved to be a blast. Dave quickly demonstrated his proficiency on the slopes of the snow-covered glaciers, so one morning he was given the chance to lead his instructor and a group of skiers down the lower front face of a glacier…

Ahead of Dave lay a dip and rise, which had concealed the terrain beyond it. Carrying about 40 miles an hour of speed over the top, he got about three feet of air, and—WOAAAH !—below and in front of him, nothing but dirt and rocks. Two days earlier, the group had skied that snowy front face; now, the snow was gone, melted by the warm summer sun of the previous days. The nearest patch of snow was way out of landing range!

Dave's skis hit the ground and he was thrown head over heels, somersaulting 45 feet across the rocks. The fall broke his right arm in two places, scratched his face, and caused a minor whiplash. Dave felt lucky to be alive.

During high school, the whiplash caused periodic stiffness in his neck and excruciating muscle spasms in his back. Still, Dave became an outstanding high school ski racer and tennis player and, as a college freshman, a varsity soccer player. His neck sometimes bothered him, but there was another more painful ache…

All throughout his teens, Dave had constantly questioned the purpose of life. Now, in college, where an assortment of tempting pleasures challenged his wholesome standards, the gnawing question screamed for an answer.

One evening Dave cried out, "Oh, God, if you are real, please somehow show Yourself, somehow communicate with me. Even a small sign or revelation, and I will come running after You."

The next day, Dave was walking through the Drew University Student Center and saw a sight that he had never seen before. Two bearded young men, wearing dark suits and black hats, were seated at a table covered with books and brochures. Dave wasn't sure who they were, but vaguely recalled the cover of a Chaim Potok novel. "Excuse me, but are you, uh, Jewish?" Dave asked.

"Hey, that's *our* question," one of them laughed. "We're students from the Rabbinical College in Morristown, and we're here to answer questions Jewish students might have about Judaism. Now, our turn: Are you Jewish?"

Dave asked questions all right. He also borrowed some books. His readings led him back on the following Friday to ask more questions. At the end of the semester, Dave transferred to Yeshiva Tiferes Bachurim in nearby Morristown. True to his deal with God, Dave put his heart and soul into yeshiva life. He immersed himself into his Jewish studies, observed traditional Jewish practices, and called himself by his Jewish name, "Dovid."

For three years, Dovid continued to be plagued by stiffness and periodic muscle spasms in his neck but this never stopped him from sitting and learning day and night. Then, one Thursday afternoon, a student tried to "adjust" Dovid's stiff back. Dovid heard a snap and felt a cold sensation where the solid young man had thrown his weight.

Feeling more discomfort than before, Dovid thanked him and returned to his studies. Later that evening, the discomfort turned into a pain which became worse and worse, until finally he had to leave the study hall and inch his way to the dormitory.

When Dovid woke up the next morning, the first attempted movement caused excruciating pain. Even small movements of his fingers sent sharp pains throughout his whole body.

During the years he had been studying in Morristown, he never bothered the Lubavitcher Rebbe about his muscle spasms. But, now, he knew he must write the Rebbe—at least for the camp kids who would be inspired by "Super Neshama" ("Super Soul"), the play that Dovid and five other students at Yeshiva Tiferes

Bachurim had been performing that summer. Dovid played the main character, Super Neshama.

What a character! Super Neshama would run all over the stage, doing all kinds of acrobatics, to escape the clutches of the big, bad *Yetzer Hara* ("the Evil Inclination"). The play was a smash hit at Jewish camps throughout New Jersey and New York. Only two performances remained for the season, but they were big ones: one in the Yeshiva's auditorium on Saturday night—in less than 36 hours!—and the final performance a week later in an auditorium in Brooklyn. Without Dovid, these performances would have to be canceled.

With excruciating pain, Dovid wrote a letter that Friday morning to the Rebbe: "May the Rebbe please give a *bracha* [blessing] that this condition should go away at least until after the final play. I don't want to complain about a little pain, but please may I at least be able to bear it and function."

That afternoon the pain got worse. Dovid stayed in his bed Friday night, and on *Shabbos* morning, still could not get out of bed. During the late afternoon, a fellow cast member came to visit him.

"No way can I do it," Dovid said to Yehuda. "You have to cancel tonight's performance."

"Don't worry, Dovid," Yehuda said. "You wrote the Rebbe. A miracle will happen."

"I don't even know if the letter even made it to the Rebbe's office, let alone reached the Rebbe's hand."

"Come on, Dovid. You know the Rebbe said he doesn't have to physically get a letter in order to 'receive' it."

"You're right," said Dovid, and made a slight nod with his head.

"Owww!" Dovid screamed.

Yehuda jumped.

"Excruciating pains shot through my body. Maybe I don't deserve such a special blessing," Dovid said, wincing with pain.

"Be strong, Dovid. *'Tracht goot vet zein goot'* [Think good, and it will be good]."

The Sabbath ended at 8:28 P.M. and the other cast members were changing into their acting outfits. Yehuda came to Dovid's room. "You gotta cancel," Dovid pleaded. "I'm not one iota better. I can't move."

"There's still time for a miracle," Yehuda said, as he rushed out of the room. The play was scheduled to start in 40 minutes.

About twenty minutes later, Dovid slightly adjusted himself in bed. He felt no pain. He slowly rolled over in his bed, again no pain. "How could it be?" he said to himself. He sat up. He stood. He walked across the room.

"It's gone, it's gone!" Dovid laughed. He jumped up and down. "It's really gone," he said, giggling like a kid.

No time to waste, Dovid put on his Super Neshama costume and ran backstage to the yeshiva's auditorium. Dovid's performance was at his best. He couldn't believe it. He felt no pain.

The next week Dovid continued to feel great. Then, on Sunday of the following week, Dovid did his crazy antics in the final play of the season, which was performed before a large crowd in Brooklyn. It was a great hit. The curtains came down… and Dovid's back stiffened.

That evening the pain and stiffness were significant, but bearable. On Tuesday morning, Dovid left Morristown and flew to Los Angeles to study in a pre-ordination program at LA's *Yeshiva Gedolah*. After telling his parents about the pain, they immediately arranged an appointment for Dovid with a top orthopedic surgeon in Los Angeles.

Dovid stiffly walked into Dr. Blassberg's office. He told the surgeon the history of his neck and back pains, and then about the Rebbe's blessing, with the pain going away just for the last two plays, and immediately afterwards, returning in part. "Uh huh, I see," said Dr. Blassberg, with a cool smile in his eye. "Let's just take an x-ray."

Lifting the developed x-ray to the light, the surgeon blurted out, "Oh, my God." He darted to a table, filled a huge syringe with a clear liquid, and headed back towards Dovid.

"One second. That's not for me!" Dovid said.

"You have a broken bone in your neck. We've got to operate right now."

"Wait one minute," Dovid said. "We aren't doing anything right now. I'm not doing anything without consulting the Rebbe."

The hidden vein on Dr. Blassberg's forehead popped out. "Are you crazy? Don't move. A spinous process is fractured. The separated piece must be removed immediately before it hits the spinal cord." He leaned closer with the syringe of cortisone.

Dovid backed away. "I made it this far with the Rebbe's blessing. Before I let anyone operate on me, I'm checking with the Rebbe."

Dr. Blassberg shook his head. "The pain and inflammation should have left you immobile. How is it possible that you have been walking around for the past two weeks? And jumping around in a play?"

"Now we both see," Dovid said with a smile, "how great a miracle it is."

Dr. Blassberg threw up his hands, slammed down the syringe, and threw up his hands again. "When you're ready for surgery, call me."

Dovid went back to the yeshiva in West Hollywood and telephoned Rabbi Groner, one of the Rebbe's secretaries. Just minutes later, Rabbi Groner called back. "The Rebbe gave you a *bracha* to be well, and said to follow the advice of a doctor who is also a friend."

The only friend Dovid had who was also a doctor was Josh Brody. Three years earlier, they had learned together in yeshiva in Morristown; Josh was now doing his medical residency in a New York City hospital. Dr. Brody told Dovid to send the x-rays to him, and he would show them to a team of top-notch orthopedic surgeons who "happened" to be temporarily stationed at his hospital.

After showing the x-rays to the orthopedic specialists, Dr. Brody called. "Dovid, no surgery. The doctors say it's too delicate an area. Their opinion is that there is a good chance that calcium deposits will form around the chip and fuse it into place."

From the Heavens to the Heart

As the weeks went by, Dovid's back healed. During the past 15 years, Dovid has not gotten even one major muscle spasm. Today, Rabbi Dovid Morris lives in Israel, with his wife Eta and their five children. But once in a while you might even see Dovid carving down the Swiss slopes.

Source: Rabbi Dovid Morris

~16~
Seeing is Believing

CHANA SORHAGEN COULD NO LONGER drive or even run her home because of her blurry eyesight. The eye drops that her opthalmologist had prescribed had not corrected the problem, so she had sought out Dr. Blumberg, a renowned eye specialist in Manhattan.

"Mrs. Sorhagen, eye surgery should correct the problem," Dr. Blumberg said. "We can schedule the surgery on March 4th, a week from Wednesday."

"Okay," Chana said to Dr. Blumberg, "I just hope it works." She knew surgery had risks and she was scared, but she could not stand having to be escorted around.

As soon as she got to her home in Morristown, New Jersey, Chana wrote a letter to the Lubavitcher Rebbe and sent it to Crown Heights via a friend. She anxiously waited two days and called the Rebbe's secretary.

"Rabbi Groner, my surgery is scheduled for next Wednesday," Chana said, with an urgent voice.

"I'll call you if there's an answer," Rabbi Groner said. "By the way, there's a group from Morristown that is scheduled to come for 'dollars' on Sunday. Why don't you come in with them?"

Chana was familiar with 'dollars'—since 1986, on his 84th birthday, the Rebbe had begun receiving thousands of people every Sunday who sought his blessings and advice. Thousands of men, women and children, Jews and Gentiles, would line up to walk past the Rebbe and receive a blessing.

The Rebbe would also hand each person a dollar, to encourage the giving of charity.

Two more days passed with no answer from the Rebbe. On Shabbos—Friday night and Saturday—Chana stayed home and had plenty of time to think. "Maybe the Rebbe didn't give me a blessing because he knows the operation will not be successful."

Chana became so anxious that she made up her mind to go to Crown Heights on Sunday.

The following day, March 1, 1992, looked as if an early Spring had moved in. The sky was a bright blue and the air felt pleasantly warm. One of the biggest crowds ever filled the sidewalk in front of 770 Eastern Parkway in Brooklyn, the Rebbe's synagogue and headquarters.

At last, Chana and the rest of the Morristown group walked past the Rebbe. The Rebbe looked at her and said, "*Bracha v'hatzlachah*" [blessing and success], and handed her a dollar.

The line monitors pulled Chana along to keep the crowd moving at a quick pace, but Chana stood firmly in front of the Rebbe. "Blessing and success" was the blessing the Rebbe said to each person in the line, but Chana felt she needed a blessing from the Rebbe specifically for the surgery.

"I am going for an eye operation on Wednesday," Chana said to the Rebbe. "I would like a *bracha*."

"For a healthy life," the Rebbe said, and handed her a second dollar.

Again, the line monitors pulled Chana along so the next person could pass by the Rebbe. Chana followed the line through the winding hallway to the sidewalk in front of 770 and found the other 25 members of the Morristown group.

"I'm so upset," Chana said to Shneur Zalman Stern, the leader of the Morristown group. "The Rebbe didn't give me a blessing for the operation."

"Chana," Shneur Zalman said, "the Rebbe gave you a blessing for 'a healthy life.' I heard him. I was standing right behind you."

"But he didn't give a blessing that the operation should be a success," Chana insisted.

Shneur Zalman smiled. "Don't be upset. 'A healthy life' presumably includes healthy eyes."

Chana was not satisfied with the answer: she knew that the Rebbe was very careful with each word he uttered, and he chose not to say that she had his blessing for a successful operation.

What should she do?

Chana knew how to make decisions. After all, when her husband passed away at age 42, she single-handedly raised her three young children and ran her husband's fledgling furniture moving business. It was a shocking change from her pleasant life as a homemaker in the suburbs and doing volunteer work for the local Hadassah chapter. But widowed, she had no choice. So she struggled and persevered, and eventually it became one of the most successful franchises in the moving industry.

Yes, Chana knew how to make decisions and how to survive in the world... but without her eyesight? It was scary. That's why she needed the Rebbe, for times like now. But his blessing did not make sense to her.

The following morning, Chana called the surgeon's office.

"What time on Wednesday does Dr. Blumberg want me to come in?"

"Mrs. Sorhagen, I was just going to call you," the nurse said. "Dr. Blumberg is not going to operate on you. He just returned from a seminar where he learned of a new drug which will totally eliminate the need for surgery. He thinks you would be a good candidate."

Chana was elated by the news. "Now I understand why the Rebbe gave me a blessing for health and not for a successful surgery," she said to herself. "Thank God for the Rebbe."

On Thursday, Dr. Blumberg re-examined Chana's eyes and told her about the new drug. After he informed her about the drug's unpleasant side effects, Chana decided not to take it. Instead, she went back to her opthalmologist of twenty years. He prescribed the same eye drops as before. This time, though, they worked. Within three weeks, Chana's eyesight was completely restored.

Chana resumed her active, independent schedule. About six weeks after receiving the dollar and blessing from the Rebbe, Chana was paying for some groceries at the local A&P. She was a dollar short. A long line of people were impatiently waiting behind her. Impulsively, she reached into a pocket of her wallet, and handed over the "Rebbe dollar." She regretted giving it away, especially because the Rebbe suffered a massive stroke the day after he handed her the dollar. But she told herself, "You'll get another one. The Rebbe will be better soon."

But Chana could not get over the loss, and felt remorse whenever she thought about it. The remorse even affected her up-beat and energetic spirit. Oh, how she wished she never gave away her dollar!

A year and a half later, in August of 1993, her son-in-law Gerry drove from New Jersey to Staten Island for business. At the Verazano Bridge, Gerry handed a $10 bill to the toll booth attendant, and tucked the receipt and change in his shirt pocket.

The following morning, Gerry unrolled the bills and saw some handwriting on one of them. "Blessing for health," it said. He was about to put the bill into his wallet, but the handwriting looked familiar.

"Hey, Bobbi," Gerry said to his wife, "doesn't this look like your mother's handwriting?"

Bobbi looked at the dollar bill. "It says 'Chana' here—that's Mom's Hebrew name. It is her handwriting!"

"Nah, that's impossible," Gerry said.

Bobbi called her mother later that afternoon, just before *Shabbos*. "You sound good for a change, Mom. What happened?"

"I don't know, but I really feel 'up.' I really feel good."

Bobbi was so happy to hear her mother sounding so good that she forgot to mention the dollar.

On Sunday morning, Bobbi called again. "Oh, Mom, I forgot to tell you. On Thursday, Gerry went through the Verazano toll and got a dollar with his change that says 'Blessing for Health' and 'Chana.' It's definitely your handwriting."

When Chana saw the dollar, she could not believe her eyes. "This is a miracle. You don't how awful I felt about giving it away."

Chana (2nd from left) with her children, Dennis, Roger, and Barbara ("Bobbi") in front of one of their company's vans

Overjoyed, Chana immediately called Rabbi Groner to tell the Rebbe that her son-in-law had received her dollar amidst his toll change.

Gerry had made a copy of the Rebbe dollar, and gladly but reluctantly returned the dollar to his mother-in-law. After all, Gerry had never received a dollar from the Rebbe. Despite his mother-in-law's urgings, he had never even seen the Rebbe in person.

About six months later, in February 1994, Gerry was paying for lunch at a delicatessen. The cashier handed him his change, and he noticed some writing on one of the bills. It looked like Hebrew or Arabic, but different from the Hebrew print found in prayer books. He showed it to his wife's uncle, and he said it was Hebrew script. On one side it said: 'Shalom Dov Ber Shapiro.' On the other side, it said, 'From the hand of the Lubavitcher Rebbe...'

Gerry shows friends a photocopy of his new "Rebbe dollar," but the original he keeps in a hidden place. After all, Gerry had never received a dollar from the Rebbe... at least not directly.

Author's note: After reading this story, Shalom Dov Ber Shapiro called to claim his lost dollar. Gerry returned it, but hopes to find another one. To this day, Chana is seeing clearly and enjoying a healthy life.

Sources: Chana Sorhagen, Gerry Grosslight, Shneur Zalman Stern

~17~
Heartbeat of a Baby

About 250 years ago, a Jewish community in Russia was suffering from a devastating epidemic. The Baal Shem Tov advised the people to write a Torah scroll. They wrote the Torah Scroll and the plague stopped.

THROUGHOUT THE NIGHT the contractions grew stronger and more frequent. Being an obstetrician, Dr. Danny Beim knew they still had plenty of time. Then, just before dawn, Danny drove his laboring wife Pam to Columbia-Presbyterian Hospital in Manhattan. Even though Pam and Danny lived in Bridgewater, New Jersey, Pam's family always used Columbia-Presbyterian because of its excellent care.

Some unexpected complications arose and towards the end of the day the doctor had to perform an emergency cesarean section. Minutes later, at 4:32 P.M., September 11, 1992, the doctor smiled and announced, "Congratulations! It's a boy."

Danny lifted his bright-faced baby up in the air and congratulated his wife, "*Mazal tov*, Pam, he's a handsome chipper."

Pam smiled faintly. The pain was well worth it. On Saturday morning, the doctor checked the baby and said he looked fine. But early Sunday morning, Pam paged a nurse. "My baby doesn't look right."

"He looks fine, Mrs. Beim," the nurse said. "Finish your breakfast and don't you worry."

After another call from Pam, a nurse came and assured the first-time mother that the baby was just fine. Pam took her post-cesarean painkillers and fell asleep. She awoke at 1 P.M. and a nurse came to the room to check her blood pressure.

"Please look at my baby," Pam whined groggily. The nurse sighed, and walked around Pam's bed and looked into the bassinet.

"Oh, my God," the nurse gasped. The baby looked ashen and was breathing rapidly. The nurse swooped up the baby and ran down the hall to the newborn nursery.

"Code!" the nurse called out, and placed an oxygen mask over the baby's face. Another nurse paged the doctor. The doctor rushed the baby to intensive care.

Shortly afterwards, Danny arrived at the hospital. He found Pam waiting in ICU next to her oxygen-masked, wired-up baby. Pam's eyes were red from crying.

Later that afternoon, the neonatologist Dr. Deena Weinstock gave the anxious parents a report. "We have to do more testing to confirm it, but it appears your baby was born with a metabolic disorder."

Danny's mouth dropped open. He knew that a newborn with a metabolic disorder (the inability to metabolize carbon dioxide and other waste products) had a very bleak prognosis.

That evening Danny's sister Betty called from her home in Queens and asked to speak to Pam. Betty worked for El Al Airlines. She always seemed to know what to say in a time of crisis. "I'm going to get you a *bracha*," Betty said.

"What does that mean?" asked Pam.

"A *bracha?* A blessing. There's a rabbi who works at Kennedy Airport who knows a special rabbi who will pray for your baby."

"Betty, I don't know how these things work. I'll leave it up to you." Pam was raised as a secular Jew. The next morning Betty went to work and saw Rabbi Yekutiel 'Kuti' Rapp at the El Al terminal. On Monday afternoon, Betty called back, "Kuti is going in right now to ask for a blessing from the Rabbi Schneerson, the Lubavitcher Rebbe."

On Tuesday morning, instead of getting needed bed rest, Pam caught a ride from her home in central New Jersey to Manhattan. Pam, who was a dentist, had already taken a leave of absence from her practice with the intention of being home for six weeks with her baby. Instead, she stayed in the hospital all day with her baby, watching the machine pump oxygen into his little body.

That evening Danny drove his wife home. "I can't live without my baby," Pam cried. "If only the doctors could find the cause."

Betty called Pam that evening to say that the Lubavitcher Rebbe gave a blessing for the baby to be well.

On Wednesday morning, Pam returned to the hospital to be with her baby. The neonatologist called Pam and Danny into her office. "We have discovered the problem. Your baby has persistent trunchus arteriosus. The trunks of the pulmonary artery and aorta are fused together."

"Oh, my God," Danny gasped. He had heard of this birth defect. The doctor explained the problem. The pulmonary artery normally carries "old," oxygen-poor blood to the lungs, and the aorta carries "new," oxygen-rich blood to the brain and the rest of the body. Now, the "old" and the "new" were mixed together, which could result in a severe lack of oxyen reaching the brain.

"Doctor, what can be done?" Pam asked. "We've got to do something to save our baby."

"If we proceed, we'll have to perform many complicated and risky operations before the baby would even be able to use his own heart. But, first," the doctor said, looking down at his chart, "we should consult with the neurologist."

That evening Danny spoke with his father, Salek Beim of Morristown, New Jersey. Six months earlier, Salek and his wife Chaya had felt as though a plague had attacked their family, with two of their three daughters suffering from lupus. So, in March 1992, just before their daughter Betty began some last-ditch chemotherapy, Salek had commissioned Rabbi Yaakov Zirkind, a *sofer* [scribe] who also lived in Morristown, to write a Torah scroll in Betty's and Ruth's merit—so that each should have a complete recovery.

The scribe immediately began the year-long project of writing a copy of the Five Books of Moses. Day after day, stroke after stroke, the highly trained scribe dipped his feather quill into a bottle of permanent black ink and wrote each letter on cowhide parchment. Each letter revealed a holy art, meticulously dictated by hundreds of rules of Torah calligraphy.

Witnessing the remarkable improvement in his sisters' health, Danny decided to become a co-sponsor with his father in the writing of the Torah scroll, in the merit that his son would live and become healthy.

Now, with the baby also in mind, the scribe continued inscribing letters in the new Torah scroll. Each letter of the Torah had to be an exacting copy of an older Torah, which had to be an exact copy of a previous Torah scroll, each one preceded by another, until the time of the writing down of the original Torah scroll by the holy hand of Moses.

On Thursday, the neurologist did an EEG on the baby. Danny had just arrived with his parents when the neurologist finished looking at the readings.

"Neurologically, it doesn't look promising," the neurologist told Danny and his parents. He explained that the heart apparently had not been able to pump enough oxygen-rich blood, which resulted in a lack of oxygen to the baby's brain.

"I'm afraid the EEG indicated extensive brain damage."

"Doctor, do you believe in miracles?" Danny's mother Chaya asked.

"Yes," he answered.

"Do you believe a miracle could happen to our grandson?" she asked.

"No. This baby will never have a miracle. He will never walk, talk…"

Later, the neonatologist advised Danny and Pam to forgo surgery and let nature take its course. "If we fix the heart, your baby may survive, but he will be institutionalized for the rest of his life," Dr. Weinstock explained.

Betty called Rabbi Rapp, who in turn gave Rabbi Leibel Groner, the Rebbe's secretary, an updated report on the baby. The Rebbe, having suffered a severe stroke six months earlier, answered yes-or-no questions posed to him by Rabbi Groner with a nod or a shake of the head.

Rabbi Rapp called Betty. "The Rebbe's answer is that the baby's brain will be okay; just fix the heart."

Fortunately, Columbia-Presbyterian Hospital where the baby was born was famous for its advanced work in neonatal heart surgery.

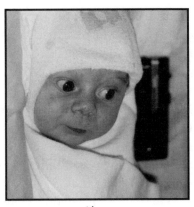

Alex

Pam and Danny called their baby Alex. He could not be given a Jewish name yet, because he was still too sick to have a *bris* [circumcision], when a Jewish boy is given his Jewish name. So every morning after the morning prayer service, Salek Beim would lead the congregation in saying a chapter of Psalms for his grandson, "Yeled ben Pessel"—"child, son of Pam." Most of his fellow congregants (which included the author of this story) did not know the details of his grandson's condition, but from the dark tones of Sal's normally cheery voice, everyone knew it had to be very grim. Some heard whispers of brain damage and other problems.

Alex had been in Columbia-Presbyterian Hospital for three weeks while the doctors evaluated his condition. "This is the worst case I have seen in 22 years of practice," said Dr. Weinstock. "You have a very sick baby. I am truly sorry, but you will never be able to take him home."

"I guess I just want a miracle for my son," Pam sobbed.

The doctor had heard Pam say that the Lubavitcher Rebbe gave a blessing to fix the heart. The neonatologist shook her head, and apparently in desperation to put reality into Pam's head, said: "I'm afraid you'll have to think about where you want your baby to die—in the hospital or in an institution."

Danny and Pam did not know what to do. As had become their habit, they called Betty who called Rabbi Rapp who gave an updated report to the Rebbe.

That evening Scott called. Scott Siegel, Danny's brother-in-law, was doing an internship in pediatric anesthesiology at the Children's Hospital of Philadelphia (CHOP).

"Danny, the world's best pediatric heart surgeons for truncus are at CHOP. Maybe you've heard of Dr. Norwood—he just made headlines for doing the surgery on the Siamese twins who were joined together at the heart. I work with him. Everyone agrees, Norwood is the world's best surgeon for truncus."

"But we can't take Alex down to Philly. Even by ambulance, it's a rough two-hour plus ride."

"I have an idea, Danny. We can fly him in a medi-copter. You and Pam discuss it and let me know what you decide."

It was too big a decision, too many unknowns. Again, they needed the Rebbe's guidance. The Rebbe was asked if they should transfer their baby to CHOP, and the Rebbe nodded in the affirmative.

Hanging onto the Rebbe's blessing, Danny and Pam agreed. A helicopter picked up Dr. Scott Siegel in Philadelphia, flew to the hospital in Manhattan, got 23-day-old Alex, and brought the doctor and his infant nephew to the rooftop of CHOP.

After two days, CHOP neurologist Dr. Robert Clancy ran an EEG on Alex. "It's not as grave as they said," Dr. Clancy told Alex's parents. "The brain wave tests must be read with different criteria for a infant than for an older child." Danny and Pam both exhaled a deep breath. Their eyes filled with tears.

"It is a bit abnormal," Dr. Clancy added. "That's to be expected. After all, as I'm sure you know, the brain is the first place that pays the price for poor circulation, as in the case with truncus. "However, I see no reason why you shouldn't operate on the heart," the neurologist concluded.

Next, heart surgeons examined Alex. "We have to do the operation as soon as possible, next Wednesday," Dr. Norwood said. The following Wednesday, October 7, was Yom Kippur. It didn't sound right to Pam and Danny to operate on the holiest day of the year. Through Betty and Rabbi Rapp, the Rebbe was consulted.

Rabbi Rapp called Betty back. "The Rebbe nodded that they should listen to the doctor. The Rebbe also said to make sure the kitchen is kosher, and that there are good *mezuzahs* on all the doors of their home."

"I'll tell Pam and Danny what the Rebbe says," Betty said, "but you know they aren't religious."

Pam told Betty that she would do anything to save her baby. Following the Rebbe's instructions, Pam bought new dishes and pots and pans and had stove made kosher, and her husband Danny affixed mezuzahs on all their doors. Alex had the surgery on the heart and it went well. Six hours afterwards there was some excess bleeding. Pam called Betty and cried to her to ask the Rebbe for one more blessing. That evening the surgeons operated on Alex again and the bleeding stopped.

On October 22, Alex came home. The parents thought he was doing all right, except that he was eating poorly. Then, on Monday, December 21, Alex was breathing rapidly, looked ashen and felt cold and clammy. They called Scott, who now lived in East Brunswick and worked as a pediatric anesthesiologist, and rushed Alex to the nearby Robert Wood Johnson Hospital emergency room in New Brunswick, New Jersey.

At one in the morning, Danny called Betty to call Rabbi Rapp. "Our baby is undergoing cardiac arrest. His heart has stopped. The doctors are now doing CPR." Betty hung up and, for a minute, debated in her mind what to do. Should she call in the middle of the night and wake up Rabbi Rapp?

"How can I not call?"

"Kuti, this is Betty, I'm sorry to wake you."

"What do you mean? I'm here only to help," Rabbi Rapp said. He took notes, got dressed, and ran to the Rebbe's office.

In the emergency room, a tiny mask fitted tightly over Alex's face, through which oxygen was being pumped. At the same time, a doctor gently pressed two of his fingers on Alex's sternum. After a half hour of doing the CPR, one of the doctors said, "Let's stop."

"Keep going," the head doctor said. CPR on an infant often takes much longer than for an adult or older child, up to an hour. The doctors kept doing CPR; a whole hour passed.

"Don't stop," said Dr. Donna Timchuk, the pediatric cardiologist. Dr. Timchuk had heard of the "amazing baby" Alex during her residency rounds at Columbia-Presbyterian Hospital. She was not going to give up so easily. Another half hour passed; suddenly, Alex revived.

An exhausted Scott exited the room. His brother-in-law and sister-in-law, who had been pacing the corridor, beseeched him with their anxious, tear-stained eyes.

"They don't expect him to survive the night," Scott said, with tears in his eyes.

Yet, Alex survived. A week later, Alex was transferred back to CHOP. They scheduled surgery for December 31, a day that was originally reserved for a New Year's eve party. Doctors Norwood and Jacobs needed to open up Alex's chest again and repeat the truncus operation.

In the days before surgery, Danny and Pam spoke directly to Rabbi Rapp for the first time. "The Rebbe said to check all mezuzahs and make sure your kitchen is kosher," Rabbi Rapp said.

"We just put mezuzahs on every door of our house two months ago," Danny said. "A young rabbi *kashered* our kitchen and made sure we put up the mezuzahs properly."

"Yes, I know," Rabbi Rapp said, "but the Rebbe said to check them. So check them again."

Danny and Pam went through the entire house making certain that every doorway had a mezuzah properly affixed to the jamb. In the basement there was a steel door leading to the garage. They looked for the mezuzah. There wasn't one! They had overlooked that door.

The next day Pam found out that the housekeeper didn't understand about the details of keeping the kitchen kosher: she had brought unkosher food into the kitchen and cooked it in the oven, thus making the oven unkosher. They had their kitchen re-kashered.

On December 31, the 15-week old Alex lay on the surgeon's table. To do the surgery, the doctors would have to cool Alex's

Avraham Chaim ("Alex") Beim with his father

body temperature down to 88 degrees. A baby can only stay at that temperature for less than two hours, so the surgery has to be completed very quickly.

With amazing dexterity and speed, Doctors William Norwood and Marshall Jacobs, divided the fused trunk of the two arteries, took tissue from his lung and, with this lung tissue, created a wall for the two newly-divided arteries.

On February 10 Alex came home. He was six months old, but weighed only 10 pounds. The parents would have to wait at least two months before Alex could undergo neurological testing of his brain.

All of this time, the scribe continued to dip his quill in the black bottle of ink, day after day, month after month, inscribing on parchment the 600,000 letters of the Torah.

Then, on July 4, 1993, under an open tent on the lawn of Congregation Ahavas Yisroel in Morristown, New Jersey, the final 250 letters of the Torah Scroll were being filled in by many friends of the Beim family. Salek Beim, the patriarch of the family, carefully filled in the last letter of the Torah, and exuberant singing erupted. The Torah scroll was rolled up and cloaked in a velvet mantle, and "danced" like a bride to her *chuppah* [wedding canopy].

Everyone—men, women, children and even babies carried in their parents' arms—kissed the new Torah. A robust, ten-month-old boy, held in the arms of his smiling father, leaned over and gave the Torah a kiss. People could not believe that this healthy-looking boy was Avraham Chaim "Alex" Beim.

Police cars arrived to escort the crowd of 200 people on the mile-long procession to the campus of the Rabbinical College of America. Men and boys danced around the wedding canopy. Dozens of mothers followed, pushing strollers and walking little children. Sussex Avenue was blocked off for half an hour while the joyous procession marched towards the Rabbinical College.

The Beim family invited everyone to a catered festive meal in the Rabbinical College's auditorium. Betty and Ruth were there with their families, and even though they were not completely cured of lupus, their conditions had improved dramatically.

Dr. Danny Beim expressed his gratitude to everyone for their prayers during that difficult year when their baby struggled for life, and how the struggle led him to believe in God.

"In April, we had brought Alex back to the Children's Hospital of Philadelphia to be examined by their top neurologist. After running a battery of tests, Dr. Clancy said, 'Your son was lucky. There's no damage to his brain.'"

"What can I say? You saw my baby today," Danny said. "My son's miraculous recovery, I attribute to the Rebbe's blessings and guidance. He's living proof that there is a God in the world."

Sources: Drs. Danny and Pam Beim; Dr. Robert Clancy of CHOP; Dr. Scott Siegel; Betty Gelbwachs; Salek Beim; Rabbi Yaakov Zirkind; Rabbi Yekutiel Rapp

~18~
Here is the Blessing

THE SWEET AROMA OF HONEY CAKE and cookies filled the air of Tzippora Vogel's apartment. Tzippora's newborn was sleeping, and two-year-old Rivka was standing at the kitchen counter, helping her mother shape a big batch of *challah* dough.

Tzippora and her husband, Aaron Yoseph, lived with their seven children on President Street on the outskirts of the Jewish section of Crown Heights, Brooklyn. In this part of Crown Heights, drug dealers called the shots. Yet Tzippora was not worried. She had a deep trust in God's benevolence, and imparted that trust to her children. They could taste it in her honey cake. They could smell it in the air. Speaking of which, the children were now on their way home. Actually, they couldn't wait to get home. Even though it was a Tuesday afternoon, *cheder* [school] was out for the rest of the week due to *Rosh Hashanah*, the Jewish New Year holiday, which would be starting the following evening.

Knock, knock.

Tzippora unlocked and opened the front door.

"Oh, *Imah* [mother], what a surprise! Come on in," Tzippora said.

"I just had a funny feeling to drop over," her mother said, almost to herself.

"Rivkie, look—Bubby's here," Tzippora announced, while bolting the door. Rivkah jumped off her chair, ran towards her Bubby and gave her a big, tight hug.

"Mmmm… Rivkie, it smells like you are baking something yummy in the oven," Bubby said.

"Cookie!" Rivkie said gleefully. Rivkie and her grandmother took the bread dough and braided some round *challahs*, while

137

Tzippora chatted in Yiddish with her mother, going over her menus for the two days of Rosh Hashanah.

Outside, the school bus stopped across the street from the Vogel's apartment, and eight-year-old Beryl excitedly skipped off the bus, full of anticipation for the coming holiday. It was 4:20 P.M.

Barely a minute passed. *Ratta tat tat!* A rapid knock rattled through the door. Tzippora quickly unlocked the door and her 7-year-old son, Levi, ran in, followed by a neighbor's daughter. "Beryleh was hit by a car!" the girl shrieked as she ran through the doorway.

"*Oy vey, Aibershter* [Oh my God]," Bubby cried out and rushed toward the door, screaming hysterically.

"Imah, calm down, everything will be all right. *Baruch Hashem*, you're here. Lock the door and watch the babies," Tzippora said as she flew out the front door toward the street.

A white Chevy van had driven around the bus, disregarding its flashing red lights, and rammed right into little Beryl, smacking right into his head. His eyeglasses and yarmulke had shot into the air, landing on the asphalt street amongst Beryl's scattered papers and Rosh Hashanah projects. One of Beryl's shoes had flown 30 feet away in the middle of the street, the other shoe landed on a street drain grid.

About 15 feet from where the van had hit him, Beryl lay motionless on his side, limp as a Raggedy Andy doll. There were no visible blood or other external signs of injury, but those who witnessed the accident knew that the boy had to be seriously injured.

A large crowd of Jewish, as well as Gentile, neighbors stood in the middle of the street. Tzipporah darted straight through the crowd and saw her son on the ground.

"Beryleh, Beryleh, it's Mama. Beryleh, Mama's here," Tzippora said, as she leaned on the ground next to her son.

No response. "Beryleh, can you hear me? Beryleh... Beryleh... Beryleh..." his mother kept repeating. Someone held her back from holding her son. "Don't touch him," warned a number of people.

"If you want your child to live, don't move him," someone said. "*Hatzalah* [the Jewish neighborhood ambulance service] is on the way."

Beryl vomited.

Now Tzippora realized that her son was very seriously injured. Over and over, she calmly whispered "Beryleh" into her son's ear. She knew the teaching of the Baal Shem Tov that whispering a person's name in the ear of a person who has fainted could draw the soul back into the body.

The police and ambulance arrived two minutes after Tzippora. The medics paged the City Ambulance to bring spinal equipment to move Beryl.

Meanwhile, two blocks away, Tzippora's husband, Aaron Yoseph, was walking home with his daughter, five-year-old Ruchama Ita. He was holding two plastic shopping bags, one of which held a new Rosh Hashanah prayer book for his son Beryl.

A boy ran past Aaron. "A boy was hit by a car, " the boy yelled to his mother who was sitting on a nearby porch.

"Tati, I'm scared," Ruchama Ita cried. Aaron Yoseph saw another boy running. "What happened?"

"A car hit one of the Vogel boys," the boy shouted as he raced by. Aaron Yoseph dropped his bags and handed Ruchama Ita to a neighbor who happened to be passing by. As he reached the scene, Beryl was being set onto a stretcher.

Tzippora was by Beryl's side, still calling out his name. The driver said they could take only one parent in the ambulance.

"A mother doesn't leave her child," Tzippora said, firmly. "Meet me at the hospital." She then looked up and asked a neighbor who was standing next to her to make sure someone would call the Rebbe's office. The neighbor answered that someone had already spoken to one of the Rebbe's secretaries.

"Beryleh, the Rebbe is praying for you. Now, I know you're in good hands," Tzippora said to her son and to herself. People in the Lubavitcher Rebbe's synagogue were already saying Psalms for Beryl. Tzippora boarded the ambulance with her son.

"Beryleh, Beryleh, can you hear me? Mama's here, Beryleh." Still, no response.

The ambulance sped to Kings County Hospital, about fifteen blocks away. In the emergency room, Tzippora continued to repeat her son's name, whispering in his ear.

"Okaaay," Beryl finally responded, as if he were saying, "Okay, Mama, I heard you, leave me alone already." But she couldn't. She wouldn't let him slip into a coma, God forbid.

"What's hurting you, Beryleh?" the mother asked.

"*Ich vesh nit* [I don't know]," he said, and then slipped back into unconsciousness.

Within ten seconds, doctors blitzed in and took over, sending Tzippora out. The corridors of the hospital quickly filled with concerned friends and relatives, as well as the media, politicians, and police brass.

The accident had occurred only 100 feet from where a Chassidic Jewish driver had accidentally and fatally struck a black child two years earlier, in August 1991, setting off the now-infamous Crown Heights riots. In response, a mob of angry black youths stabbed to death Yankel Rosenbaum, an unsuspecting Jewish student from Australia. Certain yet-to-be-accused "leaders" had incited an angry crowd. A riot ensued and bus loads of imported mobs terrorized, attacked and "vented their anger" on Jewish men, women and children in Crown Heights. Finally, after three nightmarish days, the police were finally given permission to restore law and order.

Now, two years after the Crown Heights pogrom, a black driver with a suspended license drove a van past a stopped school bus with flashing lights and struck a Jewish child. This time the police were alerted to ensure that the Jews would not 'vent' their anger and riot.

The Vogel's brother-in-law, Rabbi Yossel Katzman, became the family's spokesman. "The family wants me to emphasize that this is not a political issue," Rabbi Katzman told the media. "They feel it was an accident. The only issue that should be raised is the safety of children getting off school buses. Too often, drivers drive right past school buses that have children loading or unloading, and the law is rarely enforced."

A reporter from the NY Post had sneaked into the emergency room where Tzippora stood waiting and praying. Tzippora agreed to speak to her.

The reporter asked Tzippora questions about her son using the past tense, as if another life had become a statistic.

"How old was—"

"Was?!" Tzippora cut her in mid-sentence, her small eyes suddenly focused on the reporter's like a laser.

"But his situation was released as seriously injured and it looks…" the reporter said, undeterred.

"We Jews believe in God, that only He decides who lives," said Tzippora, her voice strong and clear. "How is it possible for you to speak like this? We believe everything will turn out well. There is still no diagnosis."

In the emergency room at Kings County Hospital, the unconscious boy was x-rayed and checked. Amazingly, the boy suffered only one broken bone—a rib. However, the CAT-scan revealed a small fracture of the skull, and internal bleeding and bruises on the brain.

Neurologists were called down to diagnose the severity of the injury. Tubes were inserted into his lungs to keep Beryl breathing, electrodes were taped to his chest to record his heartbeat, and a bolt was drilled into the skull to monitor the pressure on the brain. The neurologists knew all too well that even one small bruise on the brain could be fatal—if the swelling increases—especially in a child, because the amount of space in a child's skull is much smaller. The doctors were also very concerned about the blood clot expanding.

Beryl's breathing, heart rate, and brain pressure were being monitored. He was heavily sedated to ensure he would not move around. The amount of pressure on the brain was elevated—fluctuating between 16 and 18 HUs (Hounsfield units). Anything above 20 was very serious. The parents watched the numbers, not knowing which way they would go. Both mother and father stayed in the hospital the entire first night.

The following day, Wednesday, was the eve of Rosh Hashanah. Almost all the Jewish doctors were taking off Thursday and Friday for the Jewish New Year and a long weekend. Many of them said they would make *mi'shebeirach* blessings in their synagogues for Beryl. There was actually little else the doctors could do. It was clear to all that everything was in God's hands.

On the eve of Rosh Hashanah, when parents and children customarily call each other to wish a good sweet year, the news was passed around—literally all over the world—to pray for Beryl *ben* [the son of] Tzippora.

From around the world, an overwhelming crescendo of heartfelt prayers were said on Rosh Hashanah for Beryl. Thousands of friends, family, and fellow Jews—in America, England, France, Australia and Israel—cried prayers and Psalms for Beryl.

On Rosh Hashanah, the Day of Judgement, the Almighty decides who will live and who will die. Beryl's life lay on the scale.

On Thursday, the first day of Rosh Hashanah, Beryl developed pneumonia. Liquid matter had gotten into his lungs, as a result of the vomiting which occurred after the accident. In such a weakened state, pneumonia was life-threatening and the doctors kept trying different medications to fight it. The battle was wearing down little Beryl.

A family member reported each new development to the Lubavitcher Rebbe. Aaron Yoseph and his wife watched the brain pressure monitor. Towards the end of the first day of Rosh Hashanah—two days after the accident—the pressure seemed to be steadily going lower. On Friday, the medical staff was still very sparse because many doctors had taken off for Rosh Hashanah. Therefore the staff wanted to wait until Monday to do a CAT-scan. But Aaron Yoseph insisted that a CAT-scan be done that very day.

The CAT-scan revealed that the bleeding in the brain had stopped. The doctor instructed the nurses to stop giving Beryl sedatives, unscrewed the monitor mounted on Beryl's skull, and removed the machinery from his lungs and mouth. Immediately, Beryl wiggled his head and his torso. Within in a minute, he slowly opened his eyes.

"Good *Yom Tov*, Beryleh," said Tzippora, with tears in her eyes. "It's Rosh Hashanah."

The mother started softly singing the Rosh Hashanah prayer, *Avinu Malkenu Chatanu Lefanecha...* ["Our Father, Our King, we have sinned before You"].

"Mama, on Rosh Hashanah, we don't say *Chatanu Lefanecha*," Beryl said. (The verse, *Chatanu Lefanecha*, "we have sinned before You," is omitted on Rosh Hashanah; that verse is said only on fast days, such as Yom Kippur.)

Tears of joy and relief flowed from Tzippora's eyes: Beryl's mind seemed to be as sharp as ever. Beryl saw the charity box and picture of the Rebbe that his parents had put in the room. He smiled. "How's the Rebbe?" Beryl asked, speaking very slowly and faintly.

"*Baruch Hashem* [thank God]," his mother answered. "The Rebbe, *zol zein gezunt* [may he be healthy], ate a Yom Tov meal yesterday." The Rebbe had suffered a severe stroke six months earlier and had eaten his first solid meal on the first day of Rosh Hashanah.

Beryl smiled and then asked, "I'm already here two days? Is it day or is it night?"

"It's the middle of the day, Beryleh," his mother said. "You're here already three days. It's the second day of Rosh Hashanah."

"*Shofar*," Beryl whispered. "Mama, can I hear the shofar?"

Beryl's father had been pacing in the waiting room, reading Psalms, and clutching a shofar, a polished ram's horn.

Tzippora jumped up and poked her head into the hall. "Aaron Yoseph, Beryleh wants to hear the shofar!" Tears filled Tzippora's eyes.

Aaron Yoseph came into Beryl's room, and softly blew the shofar for his son with all his heart and soul. Now that Tzippora saw that Beryl's mind was working, she knew that pneumonia was the main danger.

On Saturday afternoon Dr. Sherman, the resident who had conscientiously worked with Beryl from the very beginning, reported to Tzippora, "Your son still has an elevated temperature." Then, with an uncharacteristic smile, Dr. Sherman added, "But he's recovering extremely fast."

That night, Tzippora spoke again to Dr. Sherman about Beryl's condition. "Mrs. Vogel, you know your son is very, very lucky," Dr. Sherman said. He was silent for a moment and then hesitatingly asked, "Have you been in touch with Rabbi Schneerson?"

"The Rebbe? Of course. The family has been in touch with the Rebbe from the very beginning," she said. Then, with a serious look, added, "Doctor, we all pray to God and God hears everyone's prayers, but the Rebbe's prayers are heard and answered."

On Tuesday, only one week after the accident, Beryl dressed himself. His shoes, which were brand new before the accident, made him realize him how lucky he was: the sole of his left shoe was rubbed paper thin by the accident. The hospital released Beryl and his father drove him home.

While Aaron Yoseph was helping his son out of the car, Beryl said, "It feels like I'm now finishing crossing the street."

Postscript: Two weeks later, after the holidays of *Sukkos* and *Simchas Torah*, classes resumed in school. Among the students was Beryl.

In November, Beryl was examined by a neurologist. "His recovery is quite amazing," said Dr. Igor Stiler of the Neurology Group of New York City, the specialist who had been monitoring Beryl's progress since he left the hospital. "We repeated the scan. There was no sign of any damage—not even a residual bruise."

Sources: Mrs. Tzippora Vogel; Dr. Igor Stiler; "Black driver runs down Jewish boy, 8, in Crown Heights," New York Post, Sept. 15, 1993.

~19~
Going for Broke

EVERY TWO TO THREE MONTHS, Max Ketch would fly from London to New York City, take a taxi cab to the Crown Heights section of Brooklyn, and sit at a Chassidic gathering with the Lubavitcher Rebbe.

Although Max knew some Yiddish from his Chassidic childhood in Poland, he was unable to follow the long, scholarly discourses of the Rebbe. But that didn't matter to Max. What Max really waited for was the break between the discourses, when the black-hatted, bearded Chassidim would sing soulful Chassidic melodies. Because then the Rebbe would invariably look across the melodious congregation of black-hatted heads, and focus his holy gaze on Max. The Rebbe would give Max a nod of recognition and a warm smile, and with a strong upward movement of his right arm, the Rebbe would wish him *"L'chaim"* [To Life].

This intimate moment would take Max out of this world, away from his everyday problems and pressures. Max would then smile with complete bliss. It was still a unique relationship in those days, in the late 1960s—a secular Jew sitting among the Chassidim at a gathering with their Rebbe. The Rebbe drew Max into his circle, onto his spiritual wings. But only for these brief moments. After all, the Rebbe's a Godly king, not a spiritual dictator.

At these gatherings, Max would always sit with his adopted Chassidic friend, Rabbi Tzvi Hersh Spritzer, a loyal follower of the Rebbe. No matter when Max appeared, Rabbi Spritzer always made room on the bench at these standing-room-only gatherings. Rabbi Spritzer considered Max his equal, as a brother, and never pried into Max's personal life. Rabbi Spritzer himself loved to hear and tell stories, especially stories about the Rebbe.

After one gathering, Max asked his friend, "Would you like to hear my story?"

Rabbi Spritzer's face lit up, and Max saw he had a captivated audience. Rabbi Spritzer's 17-year old son Shmuel, who was sitting on his father's left side, leaned forward to hear every word. Shmuel engraved in his memory the following words of Max:

Ten years ago I met Rabbi Sudak, who you know is the head Lubavitch emissary in London. Like many of the rabbis, Rabbi Sudak would come to me for donations. In exchange, he would always tell me a story of the Rebbe. Eventually, Rabbi Sudak suggested that I go to see the Rebbe, and when I did, I had the honor of having a private meeting with him. After chatting, the Rebbe asked: "Would you like to be my partner in a business deal?"

Being from a Chassidic background and knowing that having a Rebbe as a "partner" guaranteed success, I jumped at the offer.

"For sure," I said.

"Do you understand what a partnership entails?" the Rebbe asked.

"Of course, all decisions are made jointly."

"We decide everything together?" the Rebbe repeated.

"Right. For instance, if I want to sell and you don't, we don't sell. Or, if you want to sell, and I don't, we don't sell. We both must agree."

"Do you agree, we must both agree?" the Rebbe asked.

"Yes, we must both agree," I repeated.

"Good. Here's $200 for my half of the partnership. Now I want you to buy a [special kind of] fur."

It was summertime, the season when we furriers buy our furs. I bought about 100 pelts of this particular fur, which by the way is found only in the United States and Canada. I then reported to the Rebbe that I had fulfilled his request.

"So few? How are we going to make a lot of money if you're going to be so timid?" the Rebbe asked. So, I went back to the suppliers in New York City, rented a cold storage vault and filled it with a thousand pelts of this fur. The suppliers were surprised that I had bought only one kind of fur, as I had always purchased a variety.

"Now the Rebbe will be proud of me," I said to myself.

"I thought you were a businessman," the Rebbe said, upon hearing about the purchase. "I expected more from you."

I took the challenge, emptied my bank accounts in America and stretched my credit to the limit. Taking a deep breath, I bought thousands of more pelts.

"Every penny I had in my American accounts I invested in those pelts, and all my credit, too," I reported to the Rebbe with nervous pride.

"A businessman doesn't know how to wire for more money from England?" the Rebbe asked, with a smile. "Surely your son can arrange more loans."

My pride was challenged. I went for broke. I put all my money into those pelts.

"Rebbe, I bought every single piece," I reported to my 'partner.' "There's no more to be found anywhere, neither in Canada nor in the States."

"Good," the Rebbe said, with a smile. "Now, we wait. Remember, we're partners. We must both agree when to sell. Go back to England and God will help."

The winter season arrived. The price of the fur dropped 10 percent. Naturally I was concerned, but I remained calm. After all, being partners with a Rebbe, I knew from my childhood, guaranteed success.

A few weeks later, the price dropped another 10 percent. I flew to the States, and saw the Rebbe walking out of 770.

"Rebbe, the price has already dropped 20 percent. Let's sell and cut our losses."

"Don't worry. God will help," the Rebbe answered.

I went back to England. The price dropped another 20 percent. I was frantic. I flew back to New York. "Rebbe, please," I pleaded. "Let me sell. I won't tell anyone about this deal."

"No, not yet. God will help," the Rebbe said.

I returned to London. The price dropped another 10 percent. I cursed the day I had ever met the Rebbe. When Rabbi Sudak came around for his annual donation, I screamed at him,

"How could the Rebbe do this to me? The Rebbe might know spiritual worlds, but he's certainly no businessman. The Rebbe has ruined me. Now, get out of here."

The price dropped another 10 percent. Not only had I spent all my money, but I had borrowed millions to buy those pelts. I had never felt so helpless in all my life. I felt like a nothing, a real fool.

As the end of winter was quickly approaching, I received a call from a fur dealer. "I'm looking for a certain fur. I hear you're the only one who has it."

This time I knew to wait. The law of supply and demand would drive the prices up. But time was running out: the pelts were in cold storage to keep them fresh, but I couldn't keep them there forever. Well, sure enough, just as the price had gone down, it shot back up. Within a month, they were back at the original price I had paid for them.

I flew to New York. "Okay, Rebbe. Let's break even. If we sell now, it's no loss and no gain, and we'll forget that this ever happened."

"Not yet. I'll let you know when to sell. God will help."

Again I returned to London, but this time with a lighter heart. The price kept climbing, quite rapidly. The price doubled. Everybody was clambering for the fur.

Then, one day, I received a call from the Rebbe's office.

"Mr. Ketch, the Rebbe said to sell."

Within 48 hours, I sold everything. I flew back to the Rebbe. "We made millions, Rebbe. To whom should I make the check for your half of the profits?"

The Rebbe responded: "The Lubavitch House in London has outgrown its quarters. They need a larger building."

"My pleasure, Rebbe. I'll give the check to Rabbi Sudak as soon as I return to London." I then added, "Rebbe, this venture was very profitable. Maybe we could do another partnership."

"No, thanks," the Rebbe said, with a smile. "You're a *shverer shutaf* [difficult partner]."

True to his word, that was the last business partnership the Rebbe offered me. But, as you see, I fly to New York every now and then, just to be in the presence of the Rebbe.

Max was also true to his word. In 1972 many Londoners purchased "bricks" for the new Lubavitcher center, but Max's contribution paid for the bulk of the new building, which, upon completion, occupied nearly an entire city block in south London.

The years passed. Shmuel Spritzer finished his yeshiva studies and became a successful businessman. His father, Rabbi Tzvi Hersh of blesssed memory, had passed away and Rabbi Shmuel Spritzer had totally forgotten about his father's friend from London.

Then, in August of 1994, Rabbi Spritzer flew to London for a nephew's wedding. While visiting the local Lubavitch elementary school he saw an inscription on the wall which read "Max Ketch House." Seeing the name, the entire story which Max had told him back in 1969 came floating before Rabbi Spritzer's eyes. Rabbi Spritzer never forgot a story and would always tell stories at his *Shabbos tish* (Sabbath table), but inexplicably this story had remained buried deep in his memory for the past 25 years.

Rabbi Spritzer has since related this story on numerous occasions and, in the Chassidic tradition of drawing a lesson from everything one hears and sees, especially from a story involving a Rebbe, Rabbi Spritzer always concludes: "There's a timely lesson to this story. In 1951, when the Rebbe accepted the leadership of Lubavitch, he declared: 'This is a partnership. Our job is to fulfill the directive of my father-in-law, the [Previous] Rebbe, which is to bring *Moshiach*. It won't be easy, it will be a very difficult road, but we're going to do it together.'"

"We have just passed the 28th day of [the month of] Nissan," Rabbi Spritzer recently said. "It is nearly eight years since [that

149

day in 1991 when] the Rebbe declared, 'I have done all I can! Now the matter is in your hands! Do everything you possibly can… to bring our righteous Moshiach.'

"My dear friends, the Rebbe has done his share of the partnership. It's our job to finish off the last touches, which is to prepare ourselves and the world to greet and accept Moshiach. Stand firm, my friends, don't sell short. In the words of the Rebbe, 'The redemption has begun!' So hang in there, keep the faith. Moshiach is already here and, in any moment, will be revealed."

Source: Rabbi Shmuel Spritzer

~20~
The Bamboo Test

EVERY OBSERVANT JEW EATS IN A SUKKAH, a branch-covered booth, during the autumn holiday of *Sukkos*, but for eight straight years Rabbi Yitzchak Greenberg and his wife Sara could not.

Rabbi Yitzchak Greenberg earned his living as a high school science teacher in the New York City public school system, and served as the "weekend" rabbi on the Sabbath and Jewish holidays at the Interboro Jewish Center in East New York. The once-Jewish neighborhood had become quite dangerous, yet the Jews remaining in the neighborhood had pure, simple faith. In the mid-Sixties, they had built a beautiful synagogue, with a stained glass skylight and colorful murals on the walls—but without windows. They also lacked a rabbi.

They offered Rabbi Greenberg the part-time position as rabbi, which he accepted. So every Friday afternoon, Rabbi and Mrs. Greenberg would leave the comfort and safety of their Oceanside, Long Island, home and move into an apartment in East New York. The rabbi and his wife fell in love with the members of the synagogue, who were all so sweet and kind, and would always ask him to say an additional *drasha*, an insightful explanation of the week's Torah portion. When Rabbi and Mrs. Greenberg would arrive in synagogue on Friday evening, everyone would stand and applaud. They deserved it! After services, as a safety precaution, the forty or so congregants, who were all middle-aged and elderly, would walk the Rabbi and his wife to their "Shabbos apartment," and afterwards to each other's homes.

During those years, one Jew after another was maimed, robbed or murdered, some in their own apartments. Nobody and nothing was safe. In the back of the synagogue, there had been a sturdy, wooden-framed sukkah. Every night during Sukkos, some youngsters who lived in the apartment building overlooking the synagogue's yard would hurl bricks and boulders onto the bamboo roof of the sukkah.

Finally, in 1985, a week before Rosh Hashanah, the synagogue's president telephoned Rabbi Greenberg, "Rabbi, we're closing the shul. We can't even get ten men for a *minyan* [the minimum quorum for communal prayer services]." The mortgage on the beautiful synagogue had been paid up, but now it simply had to be abandoned.

Sad as he was to see the synagogue close down, Rabbi Greenberg was so happy to finally have the chance to build his own sukkah. And what a perfect location: on the patio of his Oceanside home, facing the waterfront. It looked gorgeous. His wife adorned the table beautifully with silver candlesticks and fine china. Rabbi and Mrs. Greenberg eagerly looked forward to the evening, when they would eat the first festival meal in their sukkah.

Just before sunset, Mrs. Greenberg lit the holiday candles. The sun dropped beyond the horizon and the sky filled with heavy, black clouds. Suddenly, lightning flashed across the sky. "Craaack!" Thunder exploded and a fierce storm whipped across the waterfront. The house shook from the violent wind.

Five minutes later the storm ended as suddenly as it had begun. Rabbi Greenberg walked onto the patio. "*Ribono Shel Olam* (Master of the universe)!" he cried. Amazingly, the sukkah was still standing, but the bamboo poles, which served as the makeshift roof, or *s'chach*, of the sukkah, had all tumbled to the ground, crashing on top of the fallen candlesticks and china. The *s'chach* is the essential feature of the sukkah, symbolizing the Clouds of Glory which covered and protected the Israelites after they left ancient Egypt and wandered for 40 years through the Sinai desert. Without the *s'chach* on top, the sukkah is not even considered a sukkah and, consequently, one is not allowed to eat in it.

The Rabbi felt dejected. It was already evening and the holiday of Sukkos had begun. The first two days of Sukkos are special

like the Sabbath, and Jewish Law forbids one to put *s'chach* on
on a sukkah durin g those days. What a disappointment! It's
enough of a test of faith when it rains on the first night of the
seven-day Sukkos holiday. Some people may even take it as a
slight, or in a humbler spirit, as a sign of God's displeasure. After
all, God invites (and commands) you to sit in His holy booth
where He says He will protect you under His Clouds of Glory—
and then He dumps water on you!

A chassid, with his trained attitude to look at every situation
in a positive light, considers a rainstorm on the Sukkos holiday
as a test from God. The chassid will show God that he loves the
mitzvah of sitting in the sukkah so much that he will joyfully eat
in the sukkah even when the rain is pouring through. But Rabbi
Greenberg did not even have this opportunity, because according
to Jewish law, his sukkah was no longer valid to eat in.

Rabbi Greenberg trudged upstairs to his study and searched
in his tomes of Jewish law. In such a case, where he had no other
sukkah to eat in, did the Law permit him to place the bamboo
back on? He found the ruling: the bamboo can only be replaced
on top of the sukkah by a non-Jew.

Where was he going to find someone tonight to fix his sukkah?
Especially one who would come out in this weather?

Rabbi Greenberg went downstairs to the kitchen, where his
wife was making a salad for the holiday meal. "We sacrificed and
suffered these past eight years not eating in a sukkah. And now
this happens!" Just then, Rabbi Greenberg recalled a story he
had heard years earlier. About 200 years ago, in a Jewish village
in Eastern Europe, the entire community chipped in money to
help a poor bridesgroom get started in a business. Following the
community's advice, the groom bought a horse and wagon and
went to the market to buy flour, which he would then sell in the
village. In the market, he bought sacks of flour with the remainder
of his money, and carefully loaded them onto the wagon. While
riding home, a violent gust of wind flipped his wagon over. All
the sacks of flour fell against the rocky ground and burst open,
and the wind blew the flour away. The young man turned upright

the empty wagon, and, feeling totally distraught, drove straight to his Rebbe.

The sad groom told the Rebbe about the terrible misfortune. After a minute of contemplation the Rebbe said, "God made that wind. I have to call Him to a *din Torah* [a court hearing]."

The Rebbe wept and pleaded the case for the groom. Minutes passed. Finally the Rebbe looked up and smiled. "You have won the case. Now, return to your village and all will be well."

On the road home, the groom's wagon got stuck in the mud. The unlucky groom took a broken branch and tried to dig out the wheel. The branch struck against something hard and he pushed it out of the mud. It was a chest! The young man pried it open and, behold, it overflowing with gold coins and jewels. After searching for its owner, a judge ruled that apparently robbers had hidden this treasure in the ground, and since there was nobody to whom he could return the treasure, the groom was allowed to keep it. The couple invested their fortune wisely, and became known throughout the land for their generosity and warm hospitality.

After recalling this poignant story, Rabbi Greenberg put his head on the table and cried. For eight years he was unable to eat a holiday meal in a sukkah because of the danger of eating outside in East New York. But, now, Rabbi Greenberg finally had the opportunity to eat in his own sukkah and God's wind had blown it down.

After intense meditation and heartfelt tears, Rabbi Greenberg lifted his head, smiling. "Dear," he said to his wife, "I feel like I won the *din Torah*."

Barely two minutes later, there was a knock on the door. A man stood at the door with a toolbox and rope.

"Robby! What are you doing here?"

"I came to fix your booth," Robby said.

Without even waiting for a response, Robby entered the house, walked through the living room and dining room, and stepped onto the patio. Rabbi Greenberg was aghast. He had not seen Robby for nine or ten years. Robby, who was not Jewish, worked as a licensed electrician for an observant Jew in Spring Valley, New York. Each time the business was going to be closed for a Jewish holiday, Robby would take the homebound train to Oceanside, Long Island, and pop into the nearby Ocean Harbor Jewish Center. There he would find Rabbi Greenberg, who at the time served as rabbi of this synagogue, and would ask the rabbi what each upcoming holiday was about.

Now, standing on the Rabbi's patio, Robby set down his toolbox and ropes, and inspected the damage to the sukkah. Rabbi Greenberg stood behind him, shaking his head in disbelief.

"Robby, you've never been to my home. How did you know where I lived?"

"I knew you lived in Oceanside, so I looked up your address in the phone book," Robby answered, while anchoring down the sukkah with ropes. Robby lived in Long Beach, which was one town over. "Now, Rabbi, if you don't mind waiting inside your house, I'll be finished in no time."

Half an hour later, Robby stepped into the house. "It's all done, Rabbi. Now, have a happy holiday."

"Robby, who sent you? How did you know to come here? You must be an angel of God."

"No, I'm no angel," Robby laughed. "During the storm, some feeling lured me to go onto my veranda. When I saw the strong winds knocking down all the booths, I said, 'I bet Rabbi Greenberg needs help.'"

Robby smiled and again wished Rabbi and Mrs. Greenberg a happy holiday.

Source: Rabbi Yitzchak and Sara Greenberg

๛21๛
The Fifth Question

O N MARCH 30, 1994, Rabbi Yitzchak Greenberg was sitting in a synagogue in Flatbush, Brooklyn. As he stood to leave, he twisted his back. The pain was so excruciating that he could not walk the three blocks to his daughter's home, where he and his wife were spending the Passover holiday.

An orthopedic doctor diagnosed the problem as a herniated disk. "If the medication doesn't make the pain bearable, then we'll have to consider surgery," Dr. Soslow said. Day after day, week after week, Rabbi Greenberg lay in his bed. He could not even get out of bed and walk the four feet to the bathroom.

Dr. Soslow examined him again. "Rabbi, I'm afraid you'll have to have surgery. It's the only thing that will help."

As a last resort, Rabbi Greenberg scheduled an appointment with a Chinese acupuncturist. The evening before the appointment, Rabbi Greenberg's brother called. "The pain is so unbearable that a person cannot live with it," Rabbi Irving confided to his brother, Rav Meir Greenberg of Paterson, New Jersey.

Rav Greenberg listened and asked some questions. He thought for a moment and concluded with his advice, saying, "If you call now, tomorrow morning you'll get out of bed and you'll be walking around. I assure you, this is going to happen."

Following his brother's advice, Rabbi Greenberg called Rabbi Groner, the Lubavitcher Rebbe's secretary, and asked him to read a request for health to the Rebbe. Rabbi Groner said he would read the note, but pointed out that he couldn't ask the Rebbe questions.

"Just please read it to him," Rabbi Greenberg pleaded to Rabbi Groner. Being a retired high school science teacher, Rabbi Greenberg understood the severity of his herniated disk, as well as the critical condition of the Rebbe. Six weeks earlier, the Rebbe had suffered a second major stroke, and ever since, had been lying in a coma. Still, as a life-long Lubavitcher, Rabbi Greenberg had witnessed many times how the Rebbe's blessings defied the "laws of Nature."

Rabbi Greenberg handed the phone to his wife, Sara. "Rabbi Groner said he would read the *kvitel* [written request] to the Rebbe. But, between me and you, I don't think it will help." After all, the Rebbe is not in the same condition as he was before the stroke, he thought to himself.

That night Rabbi Greenberg took his regular medicine for the excruciating pain, and eventually fell asleep. He never looked forward to the mornings, when the pain and stiffness were at its worst.

The next morning Rabbi Greenberg awoke. "Oooh, there's no pain." He got dressed, and walked up and down the block. "I feel perfect, as if nothing ever happened," Rabbi Greenberg told his wife. He canceled his appointment with the acupuncturist, and instead visited Dr. Soslow to find out if he was really all right. "If you are happy the way you are, then you don't need surgery," Dr. Soslow said.

The next Passover rolled around and Rabbi Greenberg told the story about the exodus from his own personal "slavery." Not just the torturous back pain, but the enslaving thought that the Rebbe needs to be so-called conscious to function a Rebbe.

"After the Red Sea split and our people escaped from Egypt, the Torah says, 'And they believed in God and in Moses, His servant' (Exodus 14:31).

"Certainly, after this experience, my belief in God and in the Moses of our generation, the Lubavitcher Rebbe, has reached new heights."

"And you have no more pain in your back?" a guest asked.

"I get along fine, thank God," said Rabbi Greenberg. "Only minor discomfort at times, but I can walk. I'm alive."

It's not one of the "Four Questions" at the Passover Seder, but his brother, Rav Greenberg, was later asked: "How were you so certain that your brother would feel fine in the morning?"

A moment of silence passed. Then, with a voice revealing restrained emotion, Rav Greenberg answered, "I knew I could trust the Rebbe."

Sources: Rabbi Yitzchak Greenberg; Rav Meir Greenberg; Rabbi Leibel Groner

~22~
The Richest Jew in Charleston

S
O YOU'VE LIVED IN CHARLESTON all your life," a visitor remarked to my father last summer. "Nope, only 82 years. I'm not finished yet."

To me, it seemed as if Dad would live forever.

But seven months later, in February of 1999, Dad was back in the Intensive Care Unit—ICU, as everyone calls it. I didn't panic and fly down right away. During the past 21 years, there were three other times when Dad was in ICU.

On June 19, 1978, on his 62nd birthday, Dad had quadruple bypass surgery. Most men his age would have retired after such a close call, but with two daughters in college, another who had just graduated high school and entering Boston University in the fall, and the youngest only nine years old, Dad had to "go back on the road." He worked the past 40 years as the traveling salesman for Jacobs Hosiery Company, the small family business managed by Uncle Melvin, Dad's college-educated older brother. Dad traveled the country roads crisscrossing South Carolina, calling on the small-town store owners. He took orders for T-shirts, hosiery, jeans, and other "dry goods". Jewish hardware, my father called it.

Dad's heart pumped blood through those bypass arteries for the next 10 years, allowing him to dance at the weddings of four of his daughters, as well as mine. It wasn't all fun and music those years. Among other worries and heartaches, my brother Charles, who was a year younger than me, suffered from manic-depression and was in and out of psychiatric hospitals. Finally, on June 16, 1988, while waiting to catch an airplane to their youngest daughter's high school graduation ceremony, a doctor friend intercepted them and told them the news. Charles' sweet, troubled soul had returned to its Maker.

Dad took the tragic news with the strength of Job and kept the hurt inside. He recited the mourner's prayer every day in synagogue for 30 days and wrote letters about the evils of cigarette smoking, which Dad felt contributed to Charles' heart attack. Dad rarely spoke about Charles directly.

About six months later, while sitting at a midday Sabbath meal, Dad was having terrible chest pains that wouldn't go away. A friend rushed Dad along with my mom to the emergency room. He was admitted to the hospital for observation. That evening, while merely lying in the hospital bed, Dad suffered a heart attack. Fortunately, he was in the hospital and was treated right away.

The following day, my sister Sharon, a resident of Crown Heights, stood in line with thousands of others to receive a blessing from the Lubavitcher Rebbe. Sharon spoke up and said that Dad had a heart attack. She asked the Rebbe for a blessing that Dad should have a complete recovery. The Rebbe responded, "We should hear good news."

I stood in the men's line that Sunday and also asked for a blessing for Dad, and the Rebbe also said to me, "We should hear good news." Then, I mentioned that Thursday marked my birthday. "You should have a happy birthday," the Rebbe said, emphasizing the word 'happy.'

On Thursday morning, Dad had regained sufficient strength for his cardiologist, Dr. Billy Grossman, to perform a heart catherization. Dr. Grossman injected dye into his heart and saw the culprit: four out of his five bypass arteries were clogged. Three vessels were totally blocked and the right coronary graft was 90% blocked.

"Without surgery he will not last more than a few days," Dr. Grossman said to my mom. "With surgery there is a possibility. But I don't believe the bypass arteries will hold. They have to be stretched over the old bypasses and there's not much room to work with. Even if the stitches hold, the arteries are likely to tear or clog up."

Mom asked Dad what he wanted to do.

162

"Tell them to go ahead," he said, groggily. The surgery was scheduled for that very afternoon. Dr. Grossman did not expect Dad to survive the surgery and told Mom to call all the children and tell us to rush home, including the youngest daughter who was learning in seminary in Israel. Thursday evening I arrived at the hospital. I'll never forget seeing Dad strapped to the bed, unconscious, pale and stiff, tubes and wires going in his nostrils and arm, patches on his chest, electrodes on his skull. He looked like a corpse. A machine was acting like a heart, pumping blood throughout his body. The doctors didn't know if the bypasses were going to work, but being hooked up to the heart machine was only a temporary fix. On Saturday, I was sitting at the Shabbos dinner table with two sisters; two other sisters had walked the two and a half miles to the hospital. My four married sisters had brought along their babies and toddlers—*kein ein hara*—seven altogether. On Shabbos, we took shifts watching the little ones and spending time at the hospital being near Dad and keeping Mom company, who remained by Dad's side.

On Saturday afternoon, a neighbor who was graciously serving us our Sabbath meal, answered the ringing phone. "Yes, yes," we could hear her say. Then after the longest minute, she hung up the phone and excitedly yelled out, "I have good news, I have good news!"

Just as the Rebbe said to both my sister and me, we heard good news. They unhooked Dad from the heart machine. Four of the five bypasses seemed to be working very nicely. On January 13, eight days after the bypass surgery, Dad came home. "God extended my lease," he said. "I feel 20 years younger."

Nine months later, Dad danced at his youngest daughter's wedding. Shortly afterwards, Dad ended his career as a traveling salesman and became a traveling *zaidy* (grandfather).

After nine years of *shepping nachas* (collecting joy), Dad felt severe chest pains. His arteries had clogged up again.

"Ruth, another bypass surgery is out of the question," Dr. Grossman said to my mom, "but we can try to open two of Isaac's coronary arteries with stents."

On October 21, 1997, after three hours of heart surgery, Dr. Grossman emerged exhausted with his tear ducts swollen with emotion. A nurse approached my mother and sister, "The doctor said he's sorry. The stent collapsed." My mom and sister stood, mouths open, not moving.

"You should take all of his belongings out of the room," the nurse said. My other sisters and I got a call to fly down immediately. It would be only a matter of hours...

My sister in Crown Heights again "asked" the Rebbe for a blessing. Sharon wrote a letter to the Rebbe and placed it in a volume of the Rebbe's holy letters and called the Ohel, the resting place of the Rebbe, requesting a blessing for a complete recovery. Sharon was expecting and could not travel. Her twin sister Naomi, who lives near me in Morristown, took her infant and rushed with me to Newark Airport.

When we arrived at the hospital in Charleston, the doctor said that the stent opened up on its own and Dad's heart had, incredibly, stabilized.

The following evening was the Jewish holiday of *Simchas Torah*, when we celebrate the receiving of the Torah by dancing with scrolls of the Torah. I walked four blocks to the synagogue and danced with the Torah in my arms, rejoicing at the miracle.

That was a year and a half ago. Now, Dad's back in ICU and I am pacing at Gate 91 in Newark Airport with an eerie feeling. I had never even considered bringing my slippers before, but this time I packed them, in case, God forbid, I would need to wear them for a week of mourning.

The last time I saw Dad was last summer, in July 1998. He stayed in my home in Morristown, New Jersey, for about a week. Actually it was the first time that he stayed with me for more than a couple of days. He was happy for me because I had finally purchased a house. My father's quite a handyman; I'm quite the opposite. Dad had to show me how to change a washer on the cold water handle of my bathroom sink. He showed me how to pop off the circular metal cover with the letter 'C' for cold. That was a revelation for me. I had no idea that doohickey comes off and that a screw hides underneath it. We spent a lot of time together in that little bathroom—Dad, me, and my 2-year-old son.

Dad always loved to fix things around the house and tinker with this and that. Fixing the swing set. Making wooden seats for it when the original seats fell apart after a dozen years of seven children and dozens of neighborhood children swinging on them. When I think of all that my father made for us children—badminton courts in the backyard, tether ball poles, basketball hoops—I am humbled, knowing that he worked Monday through Friday, sleeping in old roadside motels or at relatives' homes all week long and, finally, pulling in the driveway on Friday afternoon, exhausted from traveling hundreds of miles, seeing and serving his customers. On Sunday mornings he worked at Jacobs Hosiery Company, replacing his samples or turning in his paperwork. It was not an easy job, for Dad or Mom.

During my teenage years, Dad would often catch me as I was running somewhere. "Herbert, hold this end steady while I cut," Dad would say. I would dutifully do so, but my heart was always somewhere else—on the beach or water skiing, or playing ball with my friends, or reading. And Dad wouldn't just cut a straight edge for the seat of the swing. He would draw a curved line with his pencil and follow the line with a hand saw, ever so slowly and carefully. (Mom always said I took after her side of the family, which included two newsletter editors and an author of several books on Southern politics.)

Back in the mid-70's when I was in college, I remember coming home for summer break and Dad had built a treehouse. I remember because our three-bedroom house was crowded with my brother and four younger sisters living at home, so I would often sleep in that treehouse, enjoying the smell of pine needles and the gentle rocking motion of the tree when a summer breeze blew.

Airports are full of so many distractions. Something about flying that makes ordinary people feel fancy, flitting their feathers, poised to take off on an exciting journey above the clouds, a world of fantasy. It's hard to focus and pray at Gate 121. The cover of New York magazine keeps beckoning me to open it. I succumb for a minute or two; I see glorious photos of more fancy people, glowing with health and cosmetic happiness.

A photo of Dad flashes through my mind. Two summers ago, at the *bar mitzvah* dinner of their second oldest grandson, Dad and Mom sat before the camera: like king and queen for a day, surrounded by all of their grandchildren—32 *keyn ain hara* in all. My eyes are drawn to Dad's face: a calm smile of true happiness. Dad never faked a smile or a frown. I don't think he even knew how. Not your typical salesman.

I want to see that smile one more time. I imagine him seeing me, whispering with his lips or eyes, "Tzvi, it's good to see you."

Dad's vision was again nearly perfect in one eye. In November, he had cataract surgery in his right eye. "It was a cinch," Dad said. He insisted on having cataract surgery on his other eye, and his eye surgeon kept discouraging him. But Dad had been preparing for the next ten years of a wonderful life, driving up the East Coast, visiting grandchildren in Baltimore, Morristown, Brooklyn, and West Hartford. Certainly, two good eyes were much better than one. Finally, three weeks ago, cataract surgery on the left eye was done. Unfortunately, he contracted a rash, and the rash turned out to be shingles. The shingles spread across his cheeks and forehead and got into his eye. The pain was excruciating. Never before had Dad complained about any pains or other discomforts. "You know how I stop thinking about my weekday worries on the Sabbath?" he would ask with a straight face. "I put on tight shoes." Whenever he had a headache, he would take two aspirins and quietly lie down. But the shingles were so painful he could hardly eat or talk.

After three days at home, Dad fell and suffered a blow to his head. An ambulance rushed him to the emergency room and he was admitted to the hospital. No medicine could stop the pain or the shingles; he lost 15 pounds and became too weak to walk on his own. The hospital released him to a "rehab institute" for a week. It was his first time in such a place. I was fearing that a nursing home

Isaac Jacobs, seated next to his wife, Ruth, and surrounded by most of their grandchildren

would be his future. But Dad could never be happy in a nursing home, with a bunch of old and sick people. What would he do? Arts and crafts? No, Dad had to do something meaningful, like repair worn out prayer books in the synagogue. People donated new prayer books and set aside the old books for burial, but Dad took them out of their resting place and gave them new life. "Do you know how much they spent on those fancy new *siddurim* [prayer books]? They got to cost at least $20 each, and they bought at least 40 of them—that's at least $800. For $20 I bought two rolls of tape, a bottle of glue, and photocopied some missing pages, and fixed every one of the prayer books."

I glance out of the window of the plane. The plane feels so solid, yet it's riding on clouds. Things are changing too fast. Up and down. Feeling better and worse and better again. Then, last Tuesday night, Dad suffered a heart attack and returned to the hospital. Dad survived the attack and was out of the danger zone. The doctors would adjust his medicine and he'd be back on his feet as soon as the medicine started knocking out the shingles.

Last night, I phoned Mom.

"Yesterday was rough," she said. "Dad was in a lot of pain. But today he felt much better. He said he didn't feel any pain. However, he was a little confused. He thought Sarah was Sharon. But, hey, I'm always mixing up their names as well."

"Me, too. How's Dad's appetite?"

I wiped the mouth of my 8-month-old son to whom I had been feeding some mashed sweet potatoes.

"He ate well. Two meals in fact. 'The turkey's a little dry,' Dad said to the nurse."

"Well, that's a good sign. Sarah told me they weren't sure if Dad suffered some brain damage, but I asked a friend who is a doctor. He called it 'sundowning.' It happens when someone's in the hospital for a long time. It will go away when he gets out, he said."

"Yes, I don't think there's damage to his brain. He's just confused some of the time. This afternoon he was looking at the ceiling and reaching up, waving his arms. 'The window's dirty,' he said to me." 'Isaac, that's not a window. It's the light fixture,' I said. He kept mumbling to his himself. One time he called out, 'Betzalel Moshe.' "

I hadn't heard Dad mention Charles—Betzalel Moshe, my only brother—in a long time.

I pressed the phone against my ear. My wife was busy wrestling our vocal 3-year-old son into pajamas.

"Do you think I should fly down tomorrow?" I asked.

"I wouldn't rush. Diane and Sarah are driving back tonight. Susan's flying in tonight. Wait till Dad's out of ICU and a little more lucid."

The following morning I called Mom at 10:30 A.M. She had already been to the hospital and back.

"This morning when I visited, Dad was staring at the ceiling and talking in a very low, mumbling voice. Then in a loud and clear voice, he said, 'Isaac Jacobs. Isaac Jacobs.' So I said, 'What do you mean, Isaac Jacobs?' Daddy pointed up. 'Someone up there is calling me.' 'Well, tell them you're not ready,' I said." Mom laughed nervously.

Hurriedly I packed a suitcase and caught this flight. Dad had mellowed out in recent years. He had transformed himself from an over-stressed father to a happy, relaxed grandfather. The last time I visited Charleston, he was giving out "Hug Me" stickers to all of the grandchildren—one of the inexpensive pleasures that he discovered later in life. What touched me was that every night before going to bed, he would say the *Shema*—"Hear O' Israel"—and then ask God to bless each of his children, grandchildren, and great grandchildren. He kept a list of all 30-plus names by his bed, just in case his memory failed him. "Some people fall asleep by counting sheep. I just say my grandchildren's names and then I'm out," he would say with pride.

When I arrived in the Charleston Airport, my parents' neighbor, Bill Novit, was there to meet me.

"I'm sorry to be the one to tell you, Tzvi. Around 1:30, your Dad had a massive heart attack…"

No, don't tell me, I screamed inside. I looked up at Bill, my mouth hanging open.

"The doctors did everything they could revive him. He was a good man. He loved his children and was very proud of all of you."

My throat tightened painfully and salty tears dropped from my eyes.

On the following afternoon at the funeral home, Rabbi David Radinsky spoke to an overflowing crowd: "Isaac was not a wealthy man in material goods but he was a very wealthy man with family. He and Ruth have had a lot of *nachas*—a lot of spiritual peace—and in this way you might say he was one of the wealthiest men in Charleston.... He and Ruth had an open house to any stranger, any visitor.... He loved to learn Torah. He might not have been a great scholar, but many times he asked very cogent and penetrating questions. Isaac was a successful man. When you have 33 grandchildren following in your ways, a legacy that will continue on for generation after generation, you have attained true wealth."

"So you lived in Charleston all your life?" the angel asked the newcomer.

"Nope, not all my life. I'm not finished yet."

Sources: Transcript of eulogy of Rabbi David Radinsky; Jeanette LeCroy, cardiac technician for Dr. Grossman; cardiologist William Grossman, MD; internist Dr. Paul Staley; Mrs. Isaac (Ruth) Jacobs; Mrs. Yosef (Sharon) Steinherz.

৵.Epilogue.৯

WHEN I WAS TRAPPED WITHOUT A LIGHT in that cave, as described in the opening story, "Where the Moon Don't Shine," it looked as if my world was about to end. But that little bit of light made all the difference between being freed from the darkness, and spending our final days trapped in that world of darkness.

Sometimes all our sources of light unexpectedly go out, and we find ourselves in a dark and frightening world. With all of our advanced technology, we are still groping in the dark, bumping into each other and hurting each other. Inner happiness, community harmony and global peace still seem elusive.

This is when we need to pay attention to the extraordinary events happening in our lives. Taking note of our own quiet experiences of serendipity points our attention to the constant workings of divine providence. These moments of recognition are signs from the heavens that warm and waken our hearts, and strengthen us when we feel weak. We need and, indeed, we seek these calls from above, because from the heavens to the heart can be very far indeed.

It is my hope that these stories shine a bit more light into the lives of my fellow "spelunkers." After all, as Chassidic philosophy teaches, "a little light dispels a world of darkness." That means, we don't actually have to fight the darkness, we just need to turn on the light and the darkness goes away automatically.

Sharing these stories with you is also my way of thanking the many people who have shared their light with me, especially those persons whom I can no longer thank in person:

My dear father Isaac Jacobs, of blessed memory, who served for me as a living example of honesty, integrity, unpretentious goodness; my dear brother Betzalel Moshe, "Charles," of blessed memory, who as a young child discovered the light and wisdom

171

of Torah, and won the hearts of many with his warmth and love; my yeshiva teachers and personal advisors, Rabbi Dovid Wichnin of blessed memory, and Rabbi Yoseph Yitzchak "Fitzie" Lipskier of blessed memory, both of whom gave their heart and soul to teach Torah and Chassidus to late-bloomers like me; and the Lubavitcher Rebbe, Rabbi Menachem Mendel Schneerson, the person who lit—and is still lighting through his teachings, emissaries, and sublime influence—the lives of countless individuals, and hence is changing the course of humanity, who is showing the world that there is a truly a God in the world. And with this thought in mind, I recall the question a team of reporters from CNN asked the Rebbe on October 20, 1991: "Can you tell us the message you have for the world about the Moshiach?" The Rebbe said, "It was printed in all the press in all countries. If you want [to] repeat to them, repeat to them: Moshiach is ready to come now. It is only from our part to do something additional in the realm of goodness and kindness."

࠾Glossary࠾

Pronunciation Guide:

a) 'ch' represents the guttural Hebrew sound 'h' similar to the 'ch' in 'lochness monster' or 'Bach'

b) 'tz' as in seltzer or chutzpah (if too difficult, replace with the 's' sound)

*NOTE: All **italicized words** are cross-referenced within this glossary. All non-English entries are Hebrew unless otherwise indicated (yid.=Yiddish; rus.=Russian). Also, plu.=plural, fem.=feminine gender, and lit.=literally. BCE stands for "before the common era," i.e., before year number one on the secular calendar, and CE stands for the common era.*

* * *

"770": the number commonly used to refer to the address of the Lubavitcher Rebbe's synagogue and Lubavitch World Headquarters at 770 Eastern Parkway, Brooklyn, New York. *(See photo, page 185)*

Aibershter (yid. "the One above"): *God* (see *Hashem*)

Abraham (or Avraham, in Hebrew): the first Jew and the first of the three forefathers; Abraham, Isaac and Jacob.

Adar: the 12th month of the Hebrew calendar, coinciding with February or March. Adar is best known for the holiday of Purim and is associated with an increase in joy, according to the Hebrew saying, "When Adar begins there is an increase in joy."

Aleichem Shalom (lit. "unto you peace"): a greeting expressed after receiving the greeting "Shalom Aleichem."

Alter Rebbe (yid. "the Elder Rebbe"): Rabbi Schneur Zalman of Liadi, White Russia (1745-1812), founder of the *Chabad-Lubavitch* movement. Among other works, he authored the Shulchan Aruch HaRav ("Code of Jewish Law of the Rav") and the *Tanya*, his magnum opus. Born and raised in a non-Chassidic area of Latvia, he became known as a child prodigy at a young age. At his *Bar Mitzvah* celebration, the greatest scholars of his region dubbed him "Rav tanna upalig." (Meaning: He is equal in stature to the scholars of the previous generations, and is entitled to disagree with them.) In 1764, Rabbi Schneur Zalman traveled to the town of Mezritch to observe the Maggid of Mezritch and his disciples. As outstanding as his Torah scholarship was, he realized that his intense service to God lacked a higher refinement, and became a close student of the Maggid of Mezritch, who was considered to be the leading Chassidic rebbe of that generation. Among the Alter Rebbe's unique contributions to Jewish scholarship was his synthesis of the intellectual approach of the non-Chassidim with the fervent spiritual approach of the Chassidim. To this day the approach he developed is still the hallmark of Chabad chassidus. The Alter Rebbe's direct paternal lineage goes back seven generations to the well-known sage, the Maharal of Prague, who was the direct descendant of great sages who traced their ancestry to David, son of Yishai, King of Israel.

amen: it is true, may it be true. The word "amen" is pronounced as an affirmation by those hearing another recite a blessing.

Baal Shem Tov ("master of the good name"): (1698-1760) founder of the Chassidic movement. He was known throughout Russia and Eastern Europe as a profound mystic who was capable of communicating his lofty wisdom to scholars and the masses alike. He was also known as a miracle worker.

baal teshuvah (lit. "master of return"; plu., baalei teshuvah): a person who returns to God, after transgressing the Torah's commandments either deliberately or out of ignorance. In everyday speech the term is used to refer to a secular Jew or Jewess who discovers his or her Jewish heritage and becomes observant of the laws of traditional Judaism. Although a person must regret and repent of his past misdeeds, Chassidic teachings frown on excessive self-berating that is often associated with repentance, and encourage each person to focus on the returning to his true source, God. The Talmud states, "In the place where a baal teshuva stands, the righteous cannot stand," highlighting the baal teshuvah's greater potential for closeness to God, compared with one who always remained in a religious environment.

bachur (plu. "bachurim"): a boy or unmarried man

bachurette: an unmarried girl

bar mitzvah (Aramaic, "son of the commandment"): When a Jewish boy turns age 13 (and a girl turns 12), he or she has the opportunity and obligation to fulfill the commandments (mitzvoth) of the Torah; the ceremony and celebration associated with this turning point.

bas: daughter, daughter of. Term used as an official means of identification for religious purposes. During one's lifetime one is generally identified together with his or her mother's name, for example 'Leah bas Sarah', meaning 'Leah, the daughter of Sarah.'

ben: son, son of. (see *bas* above) In the case of being called up to the Torah reading, the father's name is used as a means of official identification such as 'David ben Abraham.' The difference between the paternal and maternal means of identification stems from the fact that one's Jewish identity is passed through the mother, and one's tribal affiliation is traced through the father.

Glossary

beis midrash ("house of study"): generally refers to a study hall where scholars and students learn Torah.

bentch: (yid.) bless (see *bracha*). "Bentch after eating" means to say a specific blessing or blessings after eating and/or drinking. Foods and drinks require different blessings, according to categories such as fruit, vegetable, grain, meat, etc.

bentch gomel: (yid. "bless kindness") After a person is saved from a potentially dangerous situation, such as a serious auto accident, surgery, crossing a sea or desert, or is freed from jail or captivity, one recites a specific blessing (which contains the word "Ha-gomel") during the Torah reading in synagogue, thanking God for His kindness.

boruch Hashem: (lit. bless the Name) blessed be God. The Talmud says a person should bless and thank God for good things, as well as for things that do not appear to be good, because everything that happens is from God and He is intrinsically good. Although the good may, at times, be concealed from our eyes, we have faith that even that which is not revealed goodness is ultimately good. In more recent times, this teaching was emphasized by the Baal Shem Tov. Whenever he asked people how their health or livelihood was, he encouraged them to preface their answer with "Boruch Hashem" or a similar expression thanking God, regardless of whether times were good, or difficult. By saying "Boruch Hashem" or some other praise of God, the Baal Shem Tov taught that God is tremendously pleased by this response, and in turn, pleases and nourishes His creations who praise Him.

bracha: blessing. One recites a blessing before eating and before the performance of many of the 613 commandments, such as lighting Sabbath candles and donning tefillin; one person may informally bless another person, as in "I give you a blessing for a safe trip." The etymology of the word, "bracha" means "to draw down." When a person recites a blessing, he or she is actually "drawing down" the blessing from God, the source of all blessings. When a *tzaddik* (a saintly person such as the Lubavitcher Rebbe) gives a blessing, it carries more potential for actualization, because such an individual is a "chariot" of God. Just as a chariot can only go where its driver directs it, so too a saintly person is totally united with God and, hence, is able to be an open channel through which God's blessings are drawn and flow to the intended recipient. Understandably, the better and closer the connection to the *tzaddik*, the easier it is to receive God's full blessing.

bris ("covenant"): usually refers to the "bris milah," the covenant of circumcision. This time honored Jewish practice dates back to our forefather Abraham. The ceremony ordinarily takes place on the eighth day following the birth of a Jewish boy, but can be performed later than that if delayed. A specially trained person called a "mohel" performs the procedure during which the foreskin is snipped and removed. During the ceremony, after the actual removal of the foreskin, the baby is given a Jewish name. This is because the soul is not fully revealed in a Jewish male until he has had a "kosher" circumcision. Unlike a boy, a girl is considered to be a ready vessel for revealing the Godly soul, her body not needing "correction." If a Jewish man has had a medical circumcision, he may still require a ritual ceremony (in which a drop of blood is taken) to effect this covenant with God.

bubby (yid.): grandmother

Chabad: the name of the Chassidic movement founded by the Alter Rebbe, Rabbi Schneur Zalman of Liadi (1745-1812); synonymous for Chabad is Lubavitch, the name of the town where the movement developed. Chabad is an acronym for three Hebrew words, "chochmah"(wisdom), "binah" (understanding), and "da'as" (knowledge). Chabad philosophy teaches one how to use these three levels of intellect to guide and arouse the emotions of love, awe, and joy in serving God.

Chabad House: an outreach center established by a representative of the Lubavitcher Rebbe to serve the spiritual and physical needs of Jewish men, women and children who choose to avail themselves of the various programs and services offered. There are more than 2000 such centers throughout the world. During the 40-plus years of his leadership, the Rebbe ensured that from Australia to Asuncion, Bangkok to Brussels, Zambia to Zaire, in every corner of the globe where Jews live or travel, a Chabad "Light House" would be nearby.

Chabadnik: one who belongs to the Chabad movement; synonymous with Lubavitcher.

challah: a loaf of fine bread baked in honor of the Sabbath and festivals, often braided. The challah that is mentioned in the Five Books of Moses refers to the commandment of separating a small piece of dough from the prepared batch before shaping and baking the individual loaves. During the time of the Holy Temple, the challah (the separated portion) was given to the priests (Cohanim) who served in the Temple. Nowadays, because the Temple has not yet been rebuilt, this portion is burned in one's oven. The commandment of taking challah is one of three which God entrusted specifically to Jewish women. The other two are lighting the Sabbath and festival candles, and the laws of *Family Purity*. If a woman or girl is not present, a man must separate challah or perform the candle lighting. By separating challah, a woman proclaims to herself and her family her belief in God as the provider of all sustenance.

Chanukah (lit. "dedication"): eight-day festival beginning on the 25th day of the Hebrew month of Kislev, usually coinciding with December or January. Chanukah commemorates the miraculous victory of a small band

Glossary

of Jews led by the brave and faithful Maccabees over the Syrians in 139 B.C.E. The legendary battles were precipitated by the efforts of Syrian King Antiochus, who tried to force the Jews to give up their beliefs and practices, particularly those of a suprarational nature, such as wearing *tefillin* and eating kosher food. During their occupation, the Syrians plundered and desecrated the Holy Temple. Following the miraculous victory of the Jews over the mighty Syrian army, the Jews immediately purged the Holy Temple of the enemy's idols and cleansed the walls and floors. They replaced the Temple's missing golden *menorah* (candelabra) with a makeshift metal menorah and began the search for some ritually pure olive oil to illuminate the menorah. One small cruse of the pure oil, bearing the unbroken seal of the High Priest, was found buried in the Temple's floor. This one-day supply of oil miraculously burned for eight days, just long enough to obtain more oil. This "spiritual" miracle (as opposed to the military one) is the primary focus of Chanukah, during which the menorah lights are kindled for eight consecutive nights in Jewish households throughout the world, beginning with one light on the first night, and an additional light being added each of the following seven nights. Chanukah is also associated with the eating of special foods cooked in oil, such as potato pancakes (*latkes*) and doughnuts, and the giving of Chanukah *gelt*, or money, to children with the intention that they should in turn give at least some of the money to the needy.

chassid (pl. "chassidim;" lit. "kind one"): one who practices *Chassidism*; defined in the *Talmud* as one who does kindness to another, regardless of potential personal harm.

Chassidism: the movement within traditional Judaism founded in White Russia by Rabbi Yisroel, the *Baal Shem Tov* (1698-1760). In addition to strict adherence to Jewish law, Chassidism stresses emotional involvement in prayer, the mystical dimension of Judaism, the power of joy and music, unconditional love for every Jew, and attachment to a *tzaddik* (saintly person), who provides leadership and guidance to his adherents.

Chassidus: chassidic thought and philosophy. Chassidic teachings aim to arouse a passionate devotion to, and awe of, God. To attempt to reach this lofty goal, Chassidic discourses often delve into the mystical dimension of Judaism, revealing the greatness of God, His love of people, and His simultaneously being transcendent of, and close to, this physical world. According to Chassidus, a person must accustom himself to perceive personal Divine Providence ("hashgacha pratis") in one's daily life and should maintain a constant awareness that God is continually recreating the universe and everything therein.

cheder (lit. "a room"): the traditional Jewish elementary school When famine forced the Jewish forefather Jacob to move his family to Egypt in search of sustenance, Jacob sent ahead his oldest son Reuven to set up a school for the children. Similarly, when the Previous Lubavitcher Rebbe, Rabbi Yosef Yitzchak Schneersohn, arrived in America in 1940, he made the establishment of Jewish education in America his foremost priority.

chossan: a bridegroom

chupah: a Jewish wedding canopy

chutzpah: (yid.) utter nerve; gall

Cohanim (singular, "Cohen"): the priestly class among Jews. Cohanim are the male descendants of the sons of Aaron (brother of Moses) of the tribe of Levi. Other male descendants of this tribe are known as Levites. In the Holy Temple, the principal job of the Cohanim was to make the sacrificial offerings and bless the people; the principal responsibilities of the Levites were to serve the Cohanim, to sing special songs during the Temple services, and to teach Torah to the people. The majority of Jews belong to the third class, known as Yisroel (Israelite), which incorporates all of the other tribes.

Crown Heights: the neighborhood in Brooklyn, New York, where the Lubavitch world headquarters are located. In the 1960s, when many Jews in Brooklyn were fleeing to the suburbs, the Rebbe issued his legal opinion that it is wrong to flee neighborhoods when it creates a potentially harmful situation to those who remain behind. The Rebbe urged Jewish residents to remain in Crown Heights, which was voted in the 1980s as the best integrated neighborhood in New York City.

daaven: (yid.) to pray *(See photo, page 199)*

einikloch: (yid.) grandchildren

Eishishock: a mostly Jewish town in Lithuania, near Warsaw, Poland. This once-flourishing Jewish community, which was decimated by the Nazis, is featured in the U.S. Holocaust Museum.

Eishishucker: a person from the town of Eishischock.

Elul: the final month on the Jewish calendar, Elul immediately precedes Rosh Hoshanah and the Ten Days of Repentance. Because of its proximity to the High Holy Days of *Rosh Hoshanah* and *Yom Kippur,* the month of Elul is devoted to making a personal inventory of oneself. When reflecting on one's character and deeds of the past year one should recognize the areas of his character and service to God which have been lacking and resolve to correct them. One should also take note of one's positive traits and look for ways to strengthen them. Through this excellent preparation, one merits a good and sweet new year, both materially and spiritually.

Glossary

emah (Heb., pronounced "ee-mah"): mother

erev: (lit. evening) the eve of; colloquially used to mean "the day preceding" According to the Jewish "anatomy" of a day, nightfall signifies the beginning of the new day. This is based on the verse, "And there was evening, and there was morning, one day" (Genesis 1:5). Therefore, if the first day of *Rosh Hoshanah* is Friday, the holiday actually begins on Thursday evening at sunset. Erev Rosh HaShanah thus refers to Thursday, in that the evening of that (secular) day is the beginning of the holiday.

exile: (Heb., "golus") Diaspora. The homeland for the Jewish people is the Land of Israel, as stated in the Five Books of Moses. When the Jewish people are not living in their homeland, and even when they are living in the Land of Israel but the Holy Temple is not standing, the Jewish people are living in exile, at least a spiritual exile. The Torah makes reference to the time when the Jewish people would be forced to leave their homeland, and temporarily live in exile. The first exile occurred after the First Holy Temple was destroyed in 423 BCE. The surviving Jews escaped, mainly to Babylon, but also to Western Europe. Seventy years later the Second Holy Temple was rebuilt and the first exile officially ended; however, many Jews did not return because of the harsh conditions prevailing in the Land of Israel. The second exile began in the year 69 CE and has lasted more than 1,900 years. According to Jewish sources, the second exile will end when the Messiah (Moshiach) gathers all the Jews from the "four corners of the earth" and brings them back to their homeland. At that time, the Third and Final Holy Temple will be rebuilt. The Lubavitcher Rebbe has said that the unexpected, miraculous, exodus of tens of thousands of Jews from the former Soviet Union was the beginning stage of the ingathering of the exiles.

family purity: ("taharat hamishpacha") the laws regarding intimate conduct of husband and wife, and the monthly immersion by married women in a special pool of water called a "mikveh." The Rebbe wrote, based on the notes of the Previous Rebbe, in the book "HaYom Yom": "On the subject of the campaign to popularize the observance of family purity in your community, ponder this deeply. Let us imagine that if God were to give you the opportunity to save a Jewish community from extinction (God forbid), you would certainly be willing to risk your life for this, and you would thank and praise Him for His great kindness in offering an opportunity of such enormous merit. The same holds true to an even greater degree with regard to the campaign for family purity; it is an endeavor which literally saves lives." There are numerous stories of women who had miscarriages, difficulties in conceiving, and other related problems, regarding which the Rebbe advised them to be careful with these laws. Subsequently, a remarkable number of these women successfully bore children. Observance of the off-and-on cycles of family purity is also known to enhance marital life.

farbrengen (yid. "bringing together"): a gathering of *Chassidim*, characterized by joining together in a spirit of brotherhood or sisterhood, where the participants share deep Chassidic insights, search their souls, and sing soulful Chassidic melodies.

freiliche (yid.): joyous

Frierdiker Rebbe (yid. "Previous Rebbe") Rabbi Yosef Yitzchak Schneersohn (1880-1950), the sixth Lubavitcher Rebbe; only son of the Rebbe Reshab, and father-in-law of the seventh Lubavitcher Rebbe, Rabbi Menachem Mendel Schneerson.

frum (yid.): religious; one who is observant of the laws of Torah

God: the Creator of the universe and everything in it. [Note: the letter 'o' is often omitted from the name "God" and replaced with a hyphen to prevent one from erasing or defacing the written name of God.] Chassidic teachings emphasize that God not only created the world during the Six Days of Creation, but constantly recreates it every moment from absolute nothingness. Parenthetically, although God is commonly referred to as "He," the Creator of male and female transcends this categorization. God encompasses both masculine and feminine characteristics, as reflected in the various names for God, some of which are masculine and others of which are feminine. In the mystical teachings of the Kabbala, God is often referred to by the feminine gender name, "Shechina" (the "In-Dwelling" or "Divine Presence").

gematria (Greek): Torah lessons derived from the numerical equivalent of Hebrew words and phrases in the Torah. In addition to other rules, each Hebrew letter has a numerical value (aleph=1, bais=2, ..., yud=10, chuf=20, lamed=30,...,koof=100, raish=200, shin=300, tuf=400).

Ger, Gerrer chassidim: Gerrer *chassidim* originated in the city of Ger, Poland. Today they constitute the most politically powerful group of chassidim in Israel.

Haddasah: an international Jewish women's organization, with local chapters throughout the world known for its many charitable projects, notably Haddasah Hospital in Jerusalem.

halachah: Jewish law The word "halacha" stems from the word "lech," which means "to walk." Jewish law teaches a Jew how to walk through all phases of life: religious observances, morality, business, interpersonal relationships, marital life, eating, and sleeping. Unlike man-made laws which may be contrary to human nature, these laws were prescribed by the Divine Designer of humans. Thus, although not always understood by man, these laws guide a person on his or her journey through life. Some laws are not explicitly stated in the Five Books of Moses, the "Written Law." While Moses was writing down the Five Books of Moses verbatim, God was explaining to Moses each law and the many reasons for them. This body of explanations comprises the "Oral Law," also known as the "Oral Torah." In terms of practical application, contradictions and questions often arise. Based on the "Thirteen Principles" of interpreting Torah law which God taught along with the Oral Law, Moses and later the Elders and Sages interpreted and applied the Written Law for the thousands of cases brought before them. These rulings became the "Halacha."

Haman: the anti-Semitic advisor to King Achashverush, king of the Persian Empire, around 360 BCE. Haman devised a plan whereby all the Jews of Persia were to be killed. The holiday of Purim celebrates the Jews victory over Haman and his nefarious plan.

Hashem (lit. "the Name"): God. Observant Jews commonly use the word "Hashem" to refer to the Creator instead of saying "God" or one of God's other holy names.

hatzalah ("saving"): refers to the emergency rescue squad or ambulance service which serves the needs of the residents in many Orthodox neighborhoods.

hatzlacha: success A common phrase used by chassidim with which to bless others is "hatzlacha rabbah,"or "much success." Although all blessings come from God, this fundamental principle does not obviate people from their obligation to exert themselves in their efforts to accomplish their goals. As explained in Chassidus, a blessing is compared to rain; although rain may fall, if one has not planted seeds and tilled the land, crops will not grow. Both human effort and rain (that is, blessings) are required to successfully bear fruit.

Havdalah (lit. "distinction"): the brief ceremony recited over a cup of wine or grape juice at the conclusion of Sabbath or a festival, to distinguish the holy day from the weekdays that follow.

Holy Temple (Heb., "Bais HaMikdosh"): The Holy Temple was built on Temple Mount in Jerusalem as a "dwelling place" for God, that is, as a place where God could be revealed. The First Temple was built by King Solomon and stood for 410 years, until God decreed that it be destroyed as a consequence for the sin of baseless hatred between Jews. Following the Temple's destruction Jews were exiled from the Land of Israel. Seventy years later , God allowed the Jews to return from Babylon where they had settled, and the Temple was rebuilt. The Second Temple lasted 420 years, until it was destroyed by the Roman Army in the year 69 CE. The Jews have been living in exile ever since. The third and final Temple will be rebuilt by the Messiah, at which time the Jewish people will return from exile, and God will finally have a permanent "dwelling place" in the world. After the rebuilding of the Temple, peace will reign throughout the world, for all nations.

kabbalah (lit. received): the esoteric secrets of the Torah. Kabbala was handed down orally and discreetly from generation to generation, hence the name "kabbala." In the second century of the Common Era, Rabbi Shimon bar Yachai recorded many of these teachings in a book called the "Zohar." Based on the verse, "In the 600th year of Noah's life... all the fountains of the great deep were opened and the windows of Heaven were opened" (Genesis 7:11), the Zohar predicted a future "flood" (Zohar 1.117a). The Zohar stated that the "Gates of Wisdom" would open in the "600th year of the sixth (millennium)" [in the 5500 year of Creation, corresponding to 1740 CE]. This coincides with the rapid developments in science and technology which fueled the Industrial Revolution. The Lubavitcher Rebbe explained that a corresponding flood of spiritual wisdom also commenced then. The *Baal Shem Tov*, the founder of the Chassidic movement, had recently emerged from his existence as a hidden mystic, and began revealing the secrets hidden in the "Zohar" to the masses . Many Torah scholars of the day vehemently opposed this practice. These opponents to chassidim, called "mitnagdim" (lit. those against), based their opposition on the accepted teaching that the secrets of the kabbalah are forbidden to be revealed, except to those who have attained a high level of Torah learning and purity. It was the contention of the Baal Shem Tov that God wanted these secrets revealed to the world-at-large, in fulfillment of the statement in the Zohar, "Through the spreading of the teachings of this book, the Messiah will be revealed."

kabbalist: one who lives with the teachings of kabbalah. A true kabbalist must, by definition, observe the Torah on a very high level, because one must be a fit and holy "vessel" to receive these esoteric, Godly teachings.

Kadosh Elyon: (lit.) supernal holiness

kashrus: the state of being kosher

kiddush (lit. "sanctification"): the blessing over a cup of wine expressing the sanctity of the Sabbath or of a festival. *(See photo, right)*

kosher (lit. "fit for use"): an adjective used to indicate that food or religious articles have met the standards required for their use by Torah law. A common misconception is that the laws of keeping kosher, or *kashrus*, evolved because certain animals were more sanitary than others. In fact, the laws of kashrus have nothing to do with these kinds of considerations. The only reason for the observance of the laws of *kashrus* is that God commanded Jews to follow these rules "so that you may be holy."

Kotel (lit. "wall"): the Western or Wailing Wall of the Temple Mount in Jerusalem. Jews consider the Kotel to be one of the holiest sites in the world; thousands of people pray at the Wall every day.

kvetch: (yid.) whine

Glossary

kiddush

l'chaim: (lit. "to life"): a toast customarily said over a small cup of wine or other alcoholic drink expressing good wishes, spiritually and physically. In the atmosphere of a *farbrengen*, Chassidim will generally "make a l'chaim" to help soften and open the heart.

Lubavitch (lit. "town of brotherly love," Russian): townlet in White Russia which was the center of Chabad Chassidism from 1813-1915. Its name became a synonym for the Chabad movement.

Lubavitcher Rebbe: Rabbi Menachem Mendel Schneerson (1902-1994), the seventh Lubavitcher Rebbe; eldest son of the saintly kabbalist, Rabbi Levi Yitzchak, chief Rabbi of Yekaterinoslav, Russia; seventh generation descendent of the Alter Rebbe, who was the seventh generation direct descendent of the Maharal of Prague, a direct descendent of King David (all from father to son); son-in-law of the Previous Rebbe. On the tenth of Shvat, 1951, the Rebbe officially accepted the mantle of leadership as the seventh leader of the Chabad-Lubavitch movement at a public farbrengen on the first anniversary of the passing of the Previous Rebbe, his much-revered father-in-law. The Rebbe began his new leadership role by reciting a chassidic discourse entitled *Basi LeGani*, the theme of which was an elaboration and explanation of the final discourse of the Previous Rebbe, focusing on the ultimate purpose of creation. The Rebbe explained that God desires that this world become a delightful garden ("Gan"), where

183

He can feel at home. From the human perspective, this means a "Messianic World," in which a righteous leader, who will be known as King Moshiach,will usher in an era of peace and Godly revelations. During the discourse, the Rebbe stated, "Our generation is the last generation of exile and the first generation of redemption." The Rebbe further clarified in subsequent talks that his all-encompassing, lifetime goal was to prepare the world for the coming of the Messiah. The Rebbe devoted the next forty years in pursuit of this ambitious goal, establishing more than 1400 Chabad institutions—yeshivas, campus and community Chabad Houses, drug rehabilitation centers, and vocational schools—to serve the physical and spiritual needs of countless Jews and Gentiles. Every year on the anniversary of his accepting the leadership as the seventh Lubavitch rebbe, the Rebbe repeated that the seventh generation, i.e., the generation under the leadership of the seventh rebbe, is the "last generation of Exile and the first generation of Redemption." Then, dramatically, the Rebbe announced in 1991 (Shabbos Parshas Naso): "The time of your Redemption has arrived!" The final message of the Rebbe is to prepare the world to greet Moshiach by encouraging all to increase in acts of kindness and true love of one's fellow. *(See photo, right)*

Machon Chana (lit. "dwelling place of Chana"): A yeshiva (seminary) for women interested in learning more about their Jewish heritage. Located in Crown Heights, Brooklyn, it is named after the Rebbetzin Chana, mother of the Lubavitcher Rebbe, Rabbi Menachem Mendel Schneerson. Machon Chana offers Sunday, vacation, and year-round programs for beginners in Judaism. For information, call 817-735-0030.

machzor: the special prayer book used for the Jewish holidays

Maggid of Mezritch (lit. "preacher of Mezritch"): Rabbi Dov Ber (d. 1772), disciple and successor of the Baal Shem Tov, and subsequently mentor to the first Lubavitcher Rebbe, known as the Alter Rebbe. The Maggid lived in the Russian town of Mezritch, but spread the teachings of the Baal Shem Tov throughout the Jewish communities of Russia and Poland.

Maharal of Prague: Rabbi Yehuda Loewy (1512?-1609). A leading rabbi, scholar and Kabbalist of his generation. The Maharal is presumed to have made at least one golem, a man-made "man" whose job was to protect the Jews in Prague. A statue of the Maharal stands at the entrance of the Jewish Quarter of Prague. To this day, the Jewish Quarter remains intact, as well as the synagogue in whose attic Yossel the Golem is buried. (The widespread stories about the "golem" are believed to have inspired the fictional story of Frankenstein. The book, "The Golem of Prague" by Gershon Winkler describes the historical details surrounding this well-known Jewish legend.)

Maimonides: Rabbi Moshe ben (son of) Maimon, also known by the acronym of his name, the Rambam (RaMBaM). Born in Spain in 1135, the Rambam became a foremost Jewish scholar, legal codifier, and leader. After fleeing

Glossary

The Lubavitcher Rebbe

770 Eastern Parkway

from persecution against Jews in Spain, Maimonides settled in Egypt where he became the royal physician. Among his written works are the philosophical tome, "Guide for the Perplexed," the monumental 14-volume compendium of Jewish law called "Mishneh Torah," many treatises on medicine which are still studied in medical schools, and countless treatises dealing with issues of his day. In 1982, the Lubavitcher Rebbe promoted the daily study of Maimonide's "Mishneh Torah." The Rebbe contended that the communal study of this compendium of Jewish law would contribute to Jewish unity, enhance a broad awareness of Jewish law, and hasten the coming of the Moshiach. The Rambam is the foremost authority in Jewish law on the subject of the messianic redemption.

Mashiach: the Messiah (see *Moshiach*)

matzah: the flat, unleavened bread eaten on Passover. Because the Jews left ancient Egypt in haste, the dough that they carried with them did not have time to rise (Exodus 12:39). When this dough was baked in the desert, flat bread or matzah was formed. In commemoration of the Exodus from Egypt, God commanded Jews to eat matzah on Passover, and to refrain from eating, or even owning, any leaven (Heb. "chometz") during the eight days of Passover (Exodus 13:7). Chassidic philosophy explains a deeper reason for eating matzah and avoiding leaven: when the Jews left ancient Egypt, the revelation of Godliness was so intense that nothing rose, not even yeast whose nature it is to rise. "Rising" symbolizes arrogance or haughtiness, the opposite of humility, which is the feeling one naturally has when one has a fully integrated awareness of God. When God reveals Himself, one's ego naturally deflates, and he or she automatically becomes connected and close to Him.

185

mazal (lit. "constellation, fortune"): Commonly used in the same sense as "luck," as in, "It was my mazal to find my bracelet."

mazal tov (lit. "good fortune"): traditional response upon hearing good news.

Melava Malka (lit. "escorting the queen"): a semi-festive meal eaten on Saturday night, after the conclusion of the Sabbath. The Sabbath is known as the "Queen," and the melava malka represents the "escorting of the (Sabbath) Queen" from the holy Sabbath day to the work week. At the melava malka, family and friends eat a light meal, drink hot tea, and learn some Torah. Among Chassidim, it is the custom to tell stories, especially stories about the famous miracle worker, the Baal Shem Tov.

menorah: a candelabrum; specifically, the seven-branched gold candelabrum which was kindled daily in the Holy Temple representing the source of spiritual light which illuminates this physical world. During the holiday of Chanukah, an eight-branched menorah is lit in each Jewish household to commemorate the miracle which occurred in those days.

mesiras nefesh (lit. "giving over of the soul"): self-sacrifice. In the literal sense, mesiras nefesh means risking one's life for the sake of doing God's will, such as in Communist Russia when Jews practiced their religion despite the risk of being sent to Siberia or even executed. In the everyday sense, mesiras nefesh was translated by the Alter Rebbe (the first Lubavitcher Rebbe) as giving up one's free will to do a mitzvah. For example, a boy who gives up the opportunity to play with friends in order to visit a sick person or otherwise help another person is said to have *mesiras nefesh*.

mi'shebarach (lit. "the One who blessed"): a blessing said during the Torah reading for someone who needs or wants something, such as a speedy recovery.

Messianic Era: The time surrounding the coming of the Messiah (see *Moshiach*)

mezuzah (lit. "doorpost"): a small parchment scroll affixed to each doorpost of a Jewish home. On the parchment is written the first two paragraphs of the *Shema Yisroel* prayer (Deut. 6:4-9, 11:13-21). *(See photo, right)*

minchah: the afternoon prayer service. This brief service corresponds to the "minchah" flour offering, which was took place every afternoon in the Holy Temple.

minyan: a quorum of ten. A minyan usually refers to the gathering of a minimum of ten Jewish men, age 13 and older, required for the performance of certain parts of the communal prayer services, such as Torah readings and recitation of the mourner's prayer, among others. One reason for this requirement is that any gathering of ten or more Jewish souls draws down the Divine presence, which gives the group the power to read the Holy Torah and perform other holy functions.

Glossary

kissing the mezuzah

mitzvah: a Divine commandment; a religious obligation. All mankind has been commanded by God to observe certain laws known as the Seven Laws of Noah; at Mount Sinai, Jews were given the "613 Commandments." The Lubavitcher Rebbe often taught that the word mitzvah is related to the word "tzavsah" which means to "connect" or "join." This indicates that when a person does a mitzvah, he or she is connecting to and joining with God. Thus, through the performance of the commandments, which are the will of God, a person connects with God.

Moshe Rabbainu: Moses our Rebbe (teacher).

Moshiach: (lit. "the anointed one") the Messiah. According to Jewish sources, the Messianic Era will be ushered in and led by a person crowned as "Melech HaMoshiach," the Messianic King. According to Maimonides, the foremost source in Jewish law regarding Moshiach and the messianic age, the Moshiach does not necessarily have to perform miracles to prove his status. Rather, Maimonides writes in his legal compendium, "Mishneh Torah" (Law of Kings 11:4), the following criteria for the identification of

Moshiach: "If a Davidic king [a direct father-to-son descendant of King David] arises, who studies Torah and observes the commandments prescribed by the Written Law and the Oral Law (see *halacha*), as his ancestor David did, and compels all of Israel to walk in [the way of Torah] and reinforces the breaches in its observance, and [he will] fight the wars of God, he is 'presumably Moshiach.' "If he succeeds [in all of the above], rebuilds the Holy Temple in its place [on Temple Mount in Jerusalem], and gathers the dispersed remnants of Israel [to the Land of Israel], he is 'definitely Moshiach.'" ['Presumably Moshiach,' or in Hebrew "bechezkas Moshiach," is a specific term in Jewish law which denotes the first stage of the revelation of Moshiach.] The Lubavitcher Rebbe made the following remarks on Shabbos Parshas Balak, 5751 (June 29, 1991) and later edited his talk ("Sefer HaSichos 5751," Parshas Balak): "According to all our Sages' predictions concerning the 'footsteps of Moshiach', our generation is the final generation of Exile and the first generation of redemption... It is certain, beyond any shadow of a doubt, that the time of redemption has arrived... For we are presently standing on the threshold of the redemption. Nonetheless, we see that it is difficult to internalize the awareness and recognition that we are literally standing at the threshold of the Messianic Era, to the extent of 'living' with Moshiach and redemption. The suggestion for this is the study of Torah on the Topics of Moshiach and re-demption, for it is within the ability of Torah to transform human nature. It is possible that one may be, heaven-forbid, 'outside' and far-removed from the concept of redemption, as far as one's own perception is concerned (since he has not yet emerged from his own internal exile). Yet, through Torah study on the topics of redemption, he uplifts himself to a 'redemption state-of-mind' and begins to live with the concept of redemption, amidst the realization and cognizance that 'Behold, here he comes!'"

motzaei Shabbos (lit. "the going out of Shabbos"): Saturday night. The Sabbath begins on Friday evening, just before sunset, and concludes on Saturday night, after three medium-sized stars have appeared in the sky. The conclusion of the Sabbath is marked by the havdalah ceremony, during which blessings are recited over a cup of wine, spices, and a multi-wick candle. Following the ceremony, many have the custom of making a special meal called a *melave malka* at which family and friends eat a light meal, drink hot tea, and learn some Torah. Among Chassidim, it is the custom to tell stories about the rebbes and other tzaddikim, especially stories about the famous miracle worker, the *Baal Shem Tov*.

nachas (lit. "satisfaction, pleasure"): Jewish nachas is considered to be particularly desirable from one's children.

nais (pl. **nissim**): *miracle*

narishkeit (yid.) : worthless nonsense

NCO (English): non-commissioned officer

Glossary

niggun (pl. **niggunim**): Chassidic melody. An integral part of chassidic life, the niggun arises from the depths of the composer's soul and is sung to arouse feelings of love and awe in order to inspire one to become closer to God and to serve Him with joy. In the book *HaYom Yom*, the Rebbe recorded: "Indeed, the classical chassidic niggunim [melodies] of our Rebbes have the quality of arousing in the heart of every Jew the so-called 'Pintele Yid,' the essence of a Jew, about which our Holy Scriptures say, 'I sleep, but my heart is awake' (Song of Songs 5:3). The meaning of this, our sages explain, is that though a Jew is 'asleep' in Exile, somewhere in his or her heart he is has an everlasting connection to God, Torah and *mitzvoth*."

Noahide Laws: (see *Seven Laws of Noah*)

observant: Refers to a Jewish person who observes the commandments of the Torah. The main hallmarks of an observant life are eating kosher food, observing the Sabbath and the Jewish Holy Days, and the laws of family purity.

Orthodox: category of Jews who observe the laws of the Torah. The term "Orthodox" was not used until modern times, following the emergence of less-observant groups within the Jewish community who were themselves categorized, i.e., Reform, Conservative, Reconstructionist, etc. Chassidic Jews are often labeled as "ultra-Orthodox," because they follow not only traditional Jewish laws, but go "beyond the letter of the Law" by performing the mitzvoth in an enhanced way.

Passover: a festival beginning on the 15th day of Nissan, (the first month of the year) commemorating the Exodus of the Jewish people from ancient Egypt. The Passover holiday, which falls in the Springtime, lasts seven days in the Land of Israel, and eight days in the Diaspora. (see *matzah*) In chassidic literature, much has been written about the deeper significance of Passover and the exodus from Egypt. In Hebrew, the word for Egypt is 'Mitzrayim', which etymologically comes from a word which means 'boundaries' or 'limitations.' The verse in the Torah which states, "A person must remember his going out of Egypt every day of his life" (Deuteronomy 16:3) also means, according to Chassidic philosophy, that each day a person must constantly strive to exceed his personal limitations and to overcome external and internal obstacles in the service of God.

Pesach: *Passover*

prophecy, prophet: A prophet is a man or a woman to whom God has granted the gift of knowing future events. In Jewish law, the word of a prophet is to be heeded and obeyed. If a prophet foretells a negative event, such as when Jonah said that Nineveh would be destroyed if the people did not repent, the event does not necessarily have to happen. It can be reversed by Divine decree if the impetus for it is removed. On the other hand, if a prophet predicts that a positive event will occur, it cannot be reversed, since unlike the prophesy of a negative event, it does not depend on the conduct of any individual or group. Throughout history, both Jewish and Gentile prophets have existed. The story of Bilaam, a Gentile prophet whom God gave awesome powers of prophecy, is recorded in the Five Books of Moses (Numbers ch.22-25). God, however, turned his curses into blessings. His prophecies are one of the main sources in the Five Books of Moses which allude to the advent of the Messiah and the rebuilding of the third and final Temple. Female prophets are also mentioned in the Torah, most notably, Miriam, the sister of Moses. Moses is considered to have been the greatest of prophets. From the time that the Jewish people entered the Land of Israel until the destruction of the Second Holy Temple in the year 69 CE, the era of prophecy flourished.

The Lubavitcher Rebbe explained that although the era of prophecy ended with the destruction of the Holy Temple, there is always at least one individual in every generation who possesses this power. On August 17, 1991, the Rebbe made a revolutionary statement during a public address. The Rebbe said: "[We] must publicize to all people of the generation, that we have merited that God has chosen and appointed a human being, one who possesses free choice, to fill the role of judge and advisor and the prophet of the generation, to issue directives and give advice..." "And [everyone must publicize his] most essential prophecy of immediate redemption. right away, 'Behold! Here comes Moshiach!'" (Shabbos Shoftim, 5751, ch.11) [In footnote 116 of this talk, the Rebbe wrote that this statement about the imminence of the coming of the Messiah is being made in his role] "Not as a sage, nor as a judge, but rather as a prophet, which means that it is certain [to be fulfilled]." [The Rebbe refers to a discourse of the Alter Rebbe where he explains that a prophet's prediction differs from a sage's prediction which will be manifested in the spiritual worlds, but may not necessarily be realized in this physical world. Rather, the Alter Rebbe explains, the prophet describes actual events which will later be manifested in the physical world.] In summary, the Rebbe prophesied: "Moshiach's coming is imminent!"

Psalms (Heb. "tehillim"): refers to the Psalms of King David. More than mere religious poetry, psalms have been recited by Jews in times of trouble and distress to elicit salvation and blessings from God. The Chabad Rebbes, especially the Previous Rebbe, encouraged the saying of psalms daily as a kind of "preventive medicine" and as "grease for the wagon wheels," to help ease one's daily life.

Purim (lit. "lots," as in "lottery"): a one-day holiday which commemorates the miraculous salvation of the Jewish people from a terrible decree in the ancient Persian Empire. Following the destruction of the First Holy Temple in Jerusalem, the Jewish people settled in the Persian Empire. Morale was at an all-time low, and the blight of assimilation had set in. Near the end of the 70-year exile, Haman, the anti-Semitic advisor to Persian King

Glossary

Achashverous, persuaded the monarch of the necessity to destroy Persia's Jewish population. Purim, or lots, refers to the method by which the date of the massacre would be selected. Mordechai, a local Jewish leader of the time, inspired his brethren to return to Torah observance. He also devised a plan with his niece, Esther, in which she would infiltrate the King's ranks by becoming close to him and gaining his confidence and sympathy. The king married Esther after which she revealed her Jewish identity to him and successfully pleaded the case for the Jewish nation. In the end, the tables were turned and the wicked Haman was hung on the very gallows he had built to hang Mordechai, who Haman had convinced the King, was a traitor. Subsequently, Queen Esther asked that the story of Purim be recorded. The Megillah is named after Esther, and not Mordechai, exemplifying the respected and elevated status of women in authentic, Torah-true Judaism.

pushke (yid.): charity box. In Jewish homes, pushkes have traditionally occupied a prominent place, in keeping with the central importance of the commandment to give charity. Although it is praiseworthy to give a lot of charity, the amount of money one donates does not determine the 'size' of the mitzvah. Rather it is simply the act of giving that is desirable. The Lubavitcher Rebbe initiated a campaign to encourage Jews everywhere to adorn their homes, especially the rooms of children, with pushkes. The Rebbe also encouraged Gentiles to observe this practice.

Rav (lit. "great"): a rabbi who is an authority on Jewish law

Reb: Mr.; an amicable title of respect for a Jewish male who is not a rabbi

Rebbe: (lit. "my teacher"): a saintly Torah leader who serves as a spiritual guide to his followers, who are known as chassidim; in this book, "the Rebbe" refers to the seventh and last Lubavitcher Rebbe. *(See photo, page 185)*

Rebbe-dollar: an American dollar bill, which the Rebbe handed to a person in order to encourage him to give charity. Any object handled by a tzadik is considered as a vessel for blessings from Above. (Talmud, Tractate Baba Basra). Upon receiving a dollar from the Rebbe, many would keep and cherish it and instead give one (or more) of their own to charity.

Rebbetzin: the wife of a rabbi or rebbe

Rebbetzin Chana, of blessed memory: the saintly mother of the Lubavitcher Rebbe, and wife of the Rebbe's father, Rabbi Levi Yitzchak Schneerson.

Rebbetzin Chaya Mushka, of blessed memory: wife of the Lubavitcher Rebbe, Rabbi Menachem M. Schneerson; one of three daughters of the Previous Rebbe, Rabbi Yosef Yitzchak Schneersohn.

redemption (Heb. "geulah"): refers to the time when the Messiah will be revealed and lead the Jews out of exile to the "Promised Land."

refuah shelemah: a complete healing. When someone hears that a person is sick, God forbid, a common Jewish response is, "She or he should have a refuah shelemah."

Rosh Hashanah (lit. "head of the year"): the New Year. Rosh Hashanah is the "Day of Judgment" for all of humanity. The first day of Rosh Hashanah is the anniversary of the creation of the first man, Adam. It also represents the day each year on which people accept and coronate God as King of the Universe. Among other things, the blowing of the shofar which takes place on Rosh Hashanah signifies this coronation. The term Rosh Hashanah, or "Head of the Year," teaches us that just as the head determines and directs the activity of the rest of the body, Rosh Hashanah affects the rest of the year. The month of Elul, which immediately precedes the Jewish New Year, is customarily devoted to preparing one's character and spirit for this awesome day (see *Elul*). Despite the serious nature of this day, Chassidic philosophy teaches that a person may conduct himself with inward confidence and joy, albeit subdued. This is based on a teaching of the *Baal Shem Tov* with regard to the first words of the Torah portion which is read on the Sabbath preceding Rosh Hashanah, *Atem nitzavim hayom*, "You stand this day" (Deuteronomy 29:9). 'This day' refers to Rosh Hashanah, the day of great judgment. *Nitzavim* means to stand firmly, teaching us that on Rosh Hashanah we may stand confident that God, who is the epitome of goodness, will bless us with a good and sweet year (not necessarily because we deserve it, but because God is good and merciful, and wants to express His love for His children.)

Rosh Yeshiva (lit. "head of the yeshiva"): the rabbi who heads a yeshiva.

Scroll of Esther (Heb. "Megillas Esther"): After the miraculous redemption of the Jewish people from destruction in Persia in 357 BCE, Queen Esther ordered that the story of the miracle be recorded in what is known as Megillas Esther. The Rabbinic Assembly recorded the story on a scroll of parchment. It is a requirement for all Jewish men and women to listen to every word of the reading of "Megillas Esther" on Purim. (See also *Purim*)

seder (lit. "order"): the service observed at the holiday dinner on the first two nights of Passover. At the Passover seder, family and friends read the story of the Exodus from ancient Egypt and follow the service in a book called the "Haggadah." Everyone, especially children, is encouraged to ask questions about the Exodus. The service is also characterized by the eating of matzo and bitter herbs (which remind one of the bitter slavery), and the drinking of four cups of wine (which represent the four redemptions from the four exiles).

Sefer Torah (lit. "book of the Torah"): the scroll of the Torah. A special scribe, called a sofer, copies the Five Books of Moses onto sheets of leather parchment, which are then sewn together into a long scroll. The scroll is rolled around two poles (the beginning of the scroll is attached to the

Glossary

dancing with a Sefer Torah

right pole, and the end is attached to the left pole). A cloth belt is tied around the waist of the rolled up scroll, and a velvet mantle covers it. Often, a silver crown adorns the top. The Sefer Torah is stored in the synagogue, in an ark, an enclosure which is usually located along the eastern wall of the room reserved for communal prayer. On the Sabbath and other occasions, the Sefer Torah is taken out of the ark and a specific portion of the Torah is read with a special melodious chant. Each Sefer Torah is a meticulous, hand-written copy of an older Sefer Torah, which was in turn a copy of an earlier Sefer Torah, going all the way back to the original one written down by the hand of Moses. During the 40 years that the Jewish people wandered in the Sinai Desert, God dictated and taught Moses each letter of the Torah. *(See photo, above)*

Seven Laws of Noah (Heb. "sheva mitzvoth b'nai Noach"): These seven basic laws, which are recorded in the Five Books of Moses, are the commandments which God gave for all people to follow. If a Gentile fulfills the seven Laws of Noah, it is said that God will reward her or him with a share in the World to Come. The seven laws are: 1) Believe in God: Do not worship idols; 2) Respect God and Praise Him: Do not blaspheme His name; 3) Respect human life: Do not murder; 4) Respect the family: Do not commit immoral acts; 5) Respect the rights and property of others: Do not steal; 6) Creation of a judicial system: Pursue justice (this includes helping those less fortunate); 7) Respect all creatures: Do not eat the flesh of an animal while it is still alive.

Shabbos (lit. "resting"): the Sabbath, the seventh day of the week Jews are obligated to observe the Sabbath as a day of "rest," because on that day God "rested" after creating the world for six days (Genesis 2:2). In this context "resting" means a cessation of creative work. Likewise, the "resting" a Jew is commanded to do on the Sabbath does not necessarily entail resting from physical labor. Rather, it connotes refraining from engaging in creative activities. The general categories of creative activities are derived from the 39 creative "works" (Heb. Melachos) which were involved in building the original Tabernacle in the desert. They include: making a fire, sewing, dyeing, cooking, tanning, building, cutting, and plowing, among others. Because of the prohibition of "making a fire," the Shabbos candles are lit before sunset on Friday. In addition to making an actual fire, turning on a light switch, using a telephone, and many other effortless, modern activities fall under the general category of "making a fire."

shaliach (lit. "agent"; pl. "shluchim"): emissary. In the Chabad-Lubavitch movement, a shaliach generally refers to an emissary of the Lubavitcher Rebbe who is involved in Jewish education and outreach. In the HaYom Yom book, the Rebbe wrote: "Every Jew must know that he is a shaliach of the Master of all, to bring into actuality, in whatever place he may be, the will of the Blessed One and His intention in creating the universe, namely, to illuminate the world with the light of Torah and avoda [working on refining one's self]. This is accomplished through performing practical mitzvoth and implanting in oneself good character traits." Gentiles have likewise been entrusted with the mission of making the world a "dwelling place for God."

Shavuos (lit. "weeks"): holiday commemorating the "Giving of the Torah" at Mount Sinai. Shavuos is celebrated on the 6th (and 7th, in Israel) day of the month of Sivan. It usually occurs in the month of May or June of the secular calendar.

shecht (lit. "slaughter"): to slaughter a kosher animal according to the requirements of Jewish law

Shema Yisroel (lit. "Hear, Israel"): The name, and first two words, of the Hebrew prayer which begins with the verse "Hear, O Israel, God is our L-ord, God is One"(Deuteronomy 6:4-9). Reciting this prayer twice daily, in the morning and evening, is one of the 613 Commandments which God instructed the Jewish people to observe. In it one declares that "God is one," a central tenet of Jewish faith.

Sheva Mitzvoth b'nai Noach: see *Seven Laws of Noah*

schlep (yid.): drag along

Glossary

Rabbi Avrohom Lipskier blowing the shofar

Shlita: an acronym for a blessing which is customarily placed after the name of a living tzadik derived from the Hebrew words for "He should live good, long years, amen."

shmurah matzah (lit. "guarded matzah"): *Passover* matzah that has been "guarded" to ensure that it does not come into contact with water or other liquids, thus becoming leaven, from the time the wheat is harvested until the matzah is baked. The book of Jewish mysticism, the Zohar, calls shmurah matzah the "food of faith" and the "food of health." Based on this teaching, the Lubavitcher Rebbe promoted the eating of shmurah matzah on Passover (as opposed to ordinary matzah), and encouraged everyone to give shmurah matzah to their fellow Jews to eat at their Passover seders.

shochet: a specially trained rabbi who slaughters kosher animals and fowl according to Jewish law.

shofar: the polished horn of a kosher animal, typically a ram's, which is blown at various times during the synagogue service of *Rosh Hashanah*, the Jewish New Year. *(See photo, above)*

shomer Shabbos: Sabbath observant. A person who is shomer Shabbos refrains from working on the Sabbath, and observes all the other laws associated with it. (See *Shabbos*)

shtetl (yid.): village and city ghettos in Eastern Europe in which Jews lived in clusters. Although this was usually because they preferred to live in a strictly Jewish environment, in some instances they were required to live in designated areas by local authorities.

shul (yid.): synagogue

sicha (lit. "a talk"; pl. "sichos"): a public address on a Torah subject. More than 50 volumes of the Lubavitcher Rebbe's sichos have been published. Many sichos are translated from the Yiddish into English and other languages, and appear weekly in print and on the Internet, via *L'chaim*, *Beis Moshiach*, and *Sichos in English*.

simcha: joy

Simchas Torah (lit."the joy of the Torah"): the one-day festival which follows Sukkos on which the Jewish people joyously celebrate the completion of the year-long reading of the Torah (see *Torah reading)*. The joy of Simchas Torah is expressed mainly through dancing with the Torah scrolls.The reason for this is because words and intellectual study cannot fully express the joy of being united with the Torah. Even though a Jew is commanded to study Torah every day, the essence of the Torah transcends mere intellectual comprehension. Although people may be at varying intellectual levels, Jews are all equal in their ability to experience and express joy. On Simchas Torah, the simplest Jew dances with the Torah in the same circle as the most learned rabbi.

smicha: rabbinical ordination

soul: the Godly emanation which enlivens every existence. Both animate and inanimate objects have a soul. In people, however, the soul is more reflective of God, as the verse states, "[Man was made] in the image of God."

sukkah (lit. "booth"): The outdoor booth in which Jews are commanded to "dwell" for the seven days of the festival of Succos (outside Israel, the festival lasts eight days). The mitzvah of "dwelling" is considered to be fulfilled by eating, learning Torah, and otherwise spending time in the sukkah. Many also consider sleeping in the sukkah to be a requirement. The main characteristic of the sukkah is its roof, which is of a temporary and permeable nature and is made of a cut, untreated, vegetative material such as tree branches or bamboo. The roof of the sukkah represents the "Clouds of Glory" which sheltered the Jewish people during their exodus from Egypt and subsequent 40-year journey in the Sinai Desert. The "Clouds of Glory" were a revelation of God's Divine Presence on earth. It is said that on each night of Sukkos one of the seven patriarchs of Judaism—Abraham, Isaac, Jacob, Joseph, Moses, King David, and King Solomon—visit the sukkah. *(See photo, right)*

Glossary

eating outside in the sukkah

Sukkos (also spelled Succos, Sukkot): the seven-day (or outside of the Land of Israel, eight-day) festival in the month of Tishrei, which follows Rosh HaShanah and Yom Kippur. During these days, Jews live in outdoor booths called sukkahs, as stated in the Torah, "In sukkahs you shall dwell seven days." (Leviticus 23:34) This festival, which the Torah calls, "The Season of Our Rejoicing," commemorates the forty years that the young Jewish nation wandered in the Sinai Desert.

tallis (plu. **talleisim**): a prayer shawl worn by men and boys. This garment has specially knotted strings attached to each of its four corners. One type of tallis is the *tallis kattan*, or "small" tallis, a four-cornered undergarment worn by men and boys after the age of three. Another type is the *tallis gadol*, or the "big" tallis. Married men, and in many communities also unmarried men and boys over the age of 13, wear this prayer shawl draped over their shoulders during the morning prayer service. *(See photo, page 199)*

talmid (fem. "talmidah", pl. "talmidim, talmidos"): student. In Jewish life, being learned is a great virtue. A Jew is supposed to study Torah daily, throughout his entire life. Unlike any other subject, the study of Torah is endless because it contains God's wisdom, which is infinite. In addition to the acquisition of Torah knowledge, which is essential to being a fully observant Jew, the study of Torah connects the intellect of a person with the infinite intellect of God.

Talmud: a 5,000-page, 20-volume collection of the "Oral Law," consisting of: the Six Orders of the "Mishnah," the in-depth explanation on each of paragraph of the Mishnah called "Gemora," commentary on the Mishna and Gemorrah by Rashi, Tosafos and other classical scholars of 11th and 12th centuries, and supracommentaries on the earlier commentaries of Rashi and Tosafos. The "Oral Law" originated at Mount Sinai 2,448 years after Creation (1313 BCE). When God transmitted each letter of the Five Books to His servant Moses, He also taught Moses the explanations of the laws. In contrast to the "Written Law" (that is, the Five Books of Moses), it was prohibited to write down the "Oral Law." These explanations were discussed, analyzed and memorized by the Jewish people during their forty years in the Desert. Later, after conquering and settling the Land of Israel, students and scholars continued to learn it. The "Oral Law" developed over the subsequent 1,200 years into a more crystallized body of knowledge called the "Mishna." The Mishna is a collection of the statements, discussions, and Biblical interpretations of the "Tanna'im," the first-generation Talmudic sages, who expounded the Law from 32 BCE, until around 189 CE, when Rabbi Judah Ha-Nasi completed the compilation of its teachings into the Six Orders of Mishnah. The Mishnah then became the basis of study for the Rabbis in the Torah academies throughout the world.

Tammuz: the fourth Hebrew month, which occurs in the summer

Tanya (lit. "it has been taught"): The cornerstone philosophical text of Chabad Chassidic philosophy. Modestly titled "Likutei Amarim" ("Collection of Sayings"), the Tanya is the magnum opus of the first Chabad Rebbe, Rabbi Schneur Zalman, known as the Alter Rebbe. The name "Tanya" is taken from the first word of this famous work.

tateh: (yid.) father

tefillin: prayer boxes, consisting of two leather boxes with a long leather strap attached to each one. One box and strap are bound to the upper "weaker" arm (the left arm for a right-handed person, the right arm for a left-handed person). The second box is placed on the forehead "between the eyes," just above the hairline. Jewish males, age 13 and older, wear the tefillin during the weekday morning prayers. *(See photo, right)*

tish: (yid. "table") A table around which people sit for a Sabbath or festive meal.

Tishrei: the name of the seventh month on the Hebrew calendar. Although Tishrei is the month in which Rosh Hashanah (the Jewish new year) occurs, it is called the "seventh month" because it is the seventh month after the Exodus from Egypt, which marks the birth of the Jewish people.

Torah (lit. "lesson, instruction"): the Five Books of Moses; also refers to the entire Jewish Law, including the Talmud and other sacred literature. The Torah is composed of both the revealed teachings, as well as the mystical

Glossary

wearing tallis and tefillin while daavening

teachings. (see *Talmud*). According to Chassidic philosophy, the Torah is the "Blueprint of Creation" and is literally the "Will and Wisdom of God."

Torah reading: The Torah is divided into weekly portions, which are read from the scroll of the Torah every Shabbos morning in synagogue. There are also briefer Torah readings on Monday and Thursday mornings, and on Jewish holidays and on Rosh Chodesh, the beginning of each month.

treif: (lit. "torn") unkosher food. The term is loosely applied to other things which are not conducive to "kosher" living.

tzaddik: (pl. **tzaddikim**; fem. sing. **tzaddeikes**): a saintly, or righteous, person who is exceptionally sensitive and spiritually gifted, from whom many solicit advice and blessings.

tzedakah: (lit. "righteousness") charity. In addition to financial contributions to worthwhile causes, the word tzedakah encompasses the idea of caring for the physically and spiritually needy in non-monetary ways, through other acts of goodness and kindness. Through the act of giving tzedakah, a person becomes a partner with God in sustaining the world and its inhabitants. According to Jewish law, every adult is required to donate at least 10% of his income to charity.

tzitzis: the woolen strings which are attached to a four-cornered garment called a *tallis*

Ur Kasdim: the town in the Biblical country of Aram where Abraham lived as a young child. Following his realization that a Creator existed, Abraham smashed his father's idols, an act for which the king had him thrown into a fiery furnace. Abraham stood in the fire for hours but miraculously was not burned.

Yalkut Shimoni (lit. "the collection by Simon"): a collection of certain "midrashim" Around 500 CE, "Yalkut Shimoni" and many other non-legalistic teachings of the Rabbis of the era of the *Talmud* were gathered into various collections known as Midrashim.

yarmulke (yid., derived from Hebrew words which mean "fear of the king"): head covering worn by Jewish males to constantly remind them that God is watching

yartzheit (yid., lit. "time of the year"): the Hebrew anniversary of a person's death. The yarzheit is traditionally observed by the immediate relatives of the deceased, each of whom lights a 24-hour candle in his or her home on the eve of the beginning of the anniversary. In addition, a male relative or a male representative of the family recites the mourner's kaddish in synagogue during each of the day's three prayer services. It is customary to spend all or part of the day studying Torah, and to give charity, and perform other acts of goodness in the merit of the departed.

yechidus: a private meeting between a rebbe and a follower

yeshar ko'ach (lit. "may you be strengthened"): phrase used colloquially to mean "thank you."

yeshiva: a Jewish school where the curriculum consists primarily of the learning of Torah.

Yid (Yid.): Jew

Yiddishkeit: Judaism

Yom Kippur: the day of atonement. Yom Kippur is considered to be the holiest day of the Jewish Year. In the Torah, it is referred to as the "Sabbath of Sabbaths." In addition to the prohibition of creative acts, as on Shabbos, there are five activities uniquely prohibited on Yom Kippur: eating and drinking, anointing oneself with perfumes or lotions, marital relations, washing the face or any part of the body, and wearing leather shoes. On this holy day, God forgives a person for transgressions committed during

Glossary

the previous year. Chassidic philosophy explains that the pure inner essence of the soul is revealed on Yom Kippur, and thus a person feels a greater sense of his own oneness with God.

Yud-Bais Tammuz: the 12th day of the month of Tammuz. This day is celebrated by Chabad chassidim as the anniversary of the release of the *Frierdiker Rebbe* from Bolshevik imprisonment in Leningrad, 1927. The Rebbe was imprisoned for the "crime" of supporting Jewish religious life in Communist Russia. Initially, he was sentenced to death, but it was later commuted, something which was rarely done at that time in Russia.

Yud Shvat: the tenth day of the month of Shvat, on which the *Friediker Rebbe* passed away, in 1950

yom tov (lit. "good day"): Jewish holy day

z'chus: merit

zaidy (yid.): grandfather

Zohar (lit. "shine"): the book of Jewish mysticism

zol zein gezunt (yid. "should be healthy"): a phrase wishing another good health which is customarily said after mentioning the name of a *tzaddik*

❧Acknowledgments❧

MUCH HEARTFELT THANKS...

...to my wife Esther, who made the irreversible mistake of telling me to broaden my mind and take an evening course at the local county college. So, in the spring of 1991, I signed up for a creative writing class, and Esther thus became the wife of a struggling writer. Esther turned out to have an excellent ear for telling when a story dragged or went off-key. Without her, this author would be singing the writer's blues.

...to all the people who shared their private stories with me, so that these stories could be shared with you. Publicizing one's personal miracles to strengthen the faith of others is one of the best ways to praise God for His many kindnesses.

...to editors Naomi Mauer of *The Jewish Press*, Yehudis Cohen of *L'Chaim* magazine, Sholom Dovid Pape of *Moshiach Times* magazine, and Rabbi Moshe Spalter of *The World of Lubavitch-Toronto*.

...to Larry DeAngelis, a "real angel," who skillfully critiqued and edited all of my stories.

...to Rav Zalman Wilschanski, Rabbi Yisroel Gordon, Rabbi Yeheskel Lebovic, and Rabbi Zalman Dubinsky, who patiently answered and clarified many points relating to Judaism.

...to all my friends in Morristown, New Jersey, who, during the beginning years of my career, lent me their typewriters and computers, printed my stories, faxed them to various publications, delivered computer disks to New York, and did countless other favors.

...a special thanks to three budding editors—Chana Feige Dukes, Rivkah Jacobs, and Shmuel Kessler—lots of success in high school and beyond; to artists Tim Jacobus, for the cover art, and Pam Rolande Hasegawa, for the loving photographs she took of my family.

...to Yael Resnick of Superscript Communications, who put all of her talents into designing and typesetting this book and the title type.

...to God and His faithful servant, the Lubavitcher Rebbe, who took a hunk of clay and granted him a blessing to write a book of stories.

...and, finally, to you, my readers. Just as a cook needs others to eat and enjoy his concoctions, a writer needs readers to read and enjoy his scribblings. Thank you.

Tzvi Jacobs

FOR THE ELEVATION OF THE SOULS OF
Reuven Sinai ben Chaim of blessed memory
Yehudis bas Yoseph of blessed memory

AND IN HONOR OF
Jacob and Annie Korn

Moshe and Devorah Korn
and their children:
Chaya Mushka
Yosef Dovber
Dina Sara
Menachem Mendel
Reuven Sinai

May we merit the complete redemption
immediately!

FROM A BOOK REVIEW:

"These stories are so exciting and inspirational that you will finish the book in one sitting. It's a 'feel good' collection of vignettes representative of the *baal teshuvah* genre of literary activity. I highly recommend it.... A fine feature of this volume is a comprehensive glossary of many Yiddish and Hebrew terms and expressions. This alone is reason to read the book."

MetroWest Jewish News; reviewed by **Dr. Wallace Green**,
Director, Jewish Education Association of MetroWest (New Jersey)

FROM THE MAILBOX AND E-MAILBOX:

"I love the book. It reads itself. Truly delicious reading."

Devorah (Mrs. Boruch) Klar, emissary of the Lubavitcher Rebbe,
West Orange, New Jersey

"By the time I finished the story about your Dad, tears were streaming down my face. Very touching. Looking forward to reading your other stories."

Alan Bookstaber, Paterson, New Jersey

"We all experience miracles in our lives, but our memories are often far too short. Your wonderful stories allow me to relive those special moments when I know that God is close and integral part of my life. Your stories are inspiring. Thank you for writing and sharing them."

Mickey Baldachin, New Providence, New Jersey

"I enjoyed reading your book very much. I was fascinated by your stories and the way you wrote them."

Chani Tarlow, age 8, Morristown, New Jersey

"Dear Isaac and Ruth, Just finished the book and really enjoyed it. Stories were fascinating and easy to understand. Will be in touch with your son soon to order some books for presents. Again thank you."

Mannuel Cohen, Moncks Corner, South Carolina

"The book arrived two days ago. I already read it and loved it. You did a beautiful job. The stories that involve you personally are wonderful. As are they all. You write beautifully. I loved your ending to the spelunking story, and can't get over your experience in the parking lot. I wonder about the photographer story, though. Is anyone so naive as to wander across 'fields' and through such neighborhoods in the middle of the night? Please send one copy to each of my sons."

Ellen Hawley, Minneapolis, Minnesota

"I like your warm style of storytelling. The day I received your book in the mail, I had some upsetting news. I could not sleep and enjoyed your stories in the middle of the night. Your stories comforted me."

Esther Vegh, Cleveland, Ohio

"Recently, my mother told me about an incredible book of short stories that she had bought for my brother and she mentioned a couple of the stories. I immediately recognized that she was referring to your book. My brother, Daniel, and the rest of the family enjoyed the book immensely. On a personal level, the book for me had such a tremendous impact. I found it while searching for something containing stories easy to get involved with and which I could somehow relate to. I could not put down the book, too caught up with the stories themselves and absorbing each word. I feel so lucky to have had read your stories as well as listen to tell your stories in person... you enlightened my heart."

Tzippy Saunders, London, England

"As a historian of the Jewish experience in the United States, I am always on the lookout for books and stories which describe the various faces of Judaism in America. From the streets of Crown Heights, Brooklyn, to the suburbs of Charleston, South Carolina, Tzvi Jacobs discovers the wonders of faith in modern times. He tells stories of miracles both divine and mundane. With innocence, wit, and wisdom, *From the Heavens to the Heart* opens a window into the fascinating world of a Lubavitcher Chassid."

Dale Rosengarten, curator, Jewish Heritage Collection,
College of Charleston Library

"Reading *From the Heavens to the Heart* was both fascinating and inspirational, and gave me a greater insight and understanding of the power of prayer and faith. Looking forward to your next book."

Michael Davis, Houston Texas

**IF YOU HAVE ANY
COMMENTS OR QUESTIONS**
about these stories, or if you would like
an autographed copy of *From the Heavens to the Heart*,
please call the author at 973-984-7622,
or send e-mail to tzvi.jacobs@pobox.com

Also, check out the author's website:
www.lebsontech.com/miracle

PHOTO CREDITS

Pamela Rolande Hasegawa:
Chanukah candles, page 79
Kiddush, page 183
Author and family, jacket flap and inside back cover

Tim Fuller:
Rabbi Wichnin, page 105

E.K. Tiefenbrun (London):
Lubavitcher Rebbe, page 185

Israel Lipelis:
Tefillin, page 199

Photo on page 25 is courtesy of *Beis Moshiach* magazine

↝About the Author↜

TZVI JACOBS was born Herbie Jacobs in 1954 in Charleston, South Carolina. His great-grandfather came off the boat in the port of Charleston 100 years earlier and was affectionately called "Jew Jacobs" by the local people of color.

Herbie served his time at the Charleston Hebrew Institute until his bar mitzvah, assimilated at the local public high school where they learned him Southern English, graduated from the University of the South in Sewanee, Tennessee, where he learned the dubious freedoms of secularism, and, after facing post–Viet Nam realism, earned a Master's degree in Public Health Epidemiology at the University of South Carolina. While earning a master's, a fellow student inspired by the Lubavitcher Rebbe led him to Yeshiva Tiferes Bachurim in Morristown, New Jersey, where he studied under Rabbi Avrohom Lipskier.

Currently, Tzvi works as a Clinical Research Scientist at Novartis Pharmaceuticals Corporation, where big miracles are squeezed into tiny pills. Tzvi and his wife Esther live in Morristown with their children: Chaya Mushke Bracha, Nechama Dina, Mariasha Miriam, Chana, Menachem Mendel, and Dovid.